W9-ARH-900

CHRISTIAN ETHICS

KNOWING CHRISTIANITY

A series edited by Dr. William Neil to provide for thinking laymen a solid but non-technical presentation of what the Christian religion is and what it has to say.

The first titles are:

THE CHRISTIAN FAITH

THE OLD TESTAMENT

THE LIFE AND TEACHING OF JESUS

GOD IN THE NEW TESTAMENT

THE EARLY CHURCH

THE CHRISTIAN FATHERS

FAITH AND PHILOSOPHY

CHRISTIANITY AND OTHER RELIGIONS

THE ATONEMENT

Christian Ethics

by

DAVID H. C. READ
D.D.

BJ
1251
R38

BJ1251.R38   ST. JOSEPH'S UNIVERSITY   STX

Christian ethics,

3 9353 00002 7134

108796

J. B. LIPPINCOTT COMPANY
PHILADELPHIA AND NEW YORK
1969

Copyright © 1968 by David H. C. Read

Printed in the United States of America
Library of Congress Catalog Card No.: 69-16962

EDITOR'S PREFACE

To judge by the unending flow of religious literature from the various publishing houses there is an increasingly large demand on the part of ordinary intelligent people to know more about what Christianity has to say. This series is designed to help to meet this need and to cater for just this kind of people.

It assumes that there is a growing body of readers, both inside and outside the Church, who are prepared to give serious attention to the nature and claims of the Christian faith, and who expect to be given by theologians authoritative and up-to-date answers to the kind of questions thinking people want to ask.

More and more it becomes clear that we are unlikely to get any answers that will satisfy the deepest needs of the human spirit from any other quarter. Present-day science and philosophy give us little help on the ultimate questions of human destiny. Social, political and educational panaceas leave most of us unpersuaded. If we are not to end our quest for the truth about ourselves and the world we live in, in cynicism and disillusionment, where else can we turn but to religion?

Too often in the past two thousand years the worst advertisement for Christianity has been its supporters and advocates. Yet alone of all the great world religions it has shown that a faith which was oriental in origin could be transplanted into the western world and from there strike root again in the east. The present identification of Christianity in the minds of Asians and Africans with European culture and western capitalism or imperialism is a passing phase. To say that no other religion has the same potentialities as a world-wide faith for everyman is neither to denigrate the God-given truth in Buddhism, Islam and the rest, nor to say that at this stage Christianity as generally practised and understood in the west presents much more than a caricature of its purpose.

Perhaps the best corrective to hasty judgment is to measure these two thousand years against the untold millions of years of man's development. Organized Christianity is still in its infancy, as is the mind of man as he seeks to grapple with truths that could only come to him by revelation. The half has not yet been told and the full implications for human thought and action of the coming of God in Christ have as yet been only dimly grasped by most of us.

It is as a contribution to a deeper understanding of the mystery that surrounds us that this series is offered. The intention is to build up over the years a library which under the general title of "Knowing Christianity" will provide for thinking laymen a solid but non-technical presentation of what the Christian religion is and what it has to say in this atomic age.

The writers invited to contribute to this series are not only experts in their own fields but are all men who are deeply concerned that the gulf should be bridged between the specialized studies of the theologian and the untheologically minded average reader who nevertheless wants to know what theology has to say. I am sure that I speak in the name of all my colleagues in this venture when I express the hope that this series will do much to bridge the gap.

WILLIAM NEIL

The University,
Nottingham

AUTHOR'S PREFACE

THIS book has grown out of the encounter of traditional Christian ethics with experience in the last few decades. It is not an academic summary of moral theology, nor does it claim to set forth some startling new approach. Its purpose is neither to instruct nor to shock, but to offer some basis for reflection upon the practical questions that concern us all in the light of the Christian Gospel. Although technical language cannot be entirely avoided these chapters are intended to be readable by those without special training in philosophy or religion. The author has tried even harder to avoid the more recent jargon of the Christian ethical debate.

My thanks are due to the Trustees of the Croall Lectureship whose kind invitation led to the substance of these chapters being delivered in Edinburgh in 1965; to the Faculty of Divinity at Edinburgh University for their hospitality on that occasion; and to my secretary, Miss Agnes Dougall, for her skilful assistance with the manuscript.

DAVID H. C. READ

New York City

CONTENTS

ACKNOWLEDGMENTS

Permission to quote from *The New English Bible*
has been granted by the Oxford and Cambridge
University Presses (copyright 1961).

Chapter One

NEW MORALITY?

ANY book dealing with Christian ethics is bound to be coloured by the society in which it appears. There are some constant features of the discussion which reappear in each generation — otherwise there would be no such thing as Christian ethics at all — but no subject is more vulnerable to the stresses and strains of the contemporary scene. For ethics is about the way people live, their ideas of right and wrong, their aspirations, their goals, their judgments of one another. Any attempt, therefore, to talk about the Christian tradition has to be made with some sensitivity to what is being said and done by all kinds of people in our world today. There is no live possibility of wrapping up the subject as a standard package of abstract truths relevant to any period of history. This book will thus treat some of the classic themes of Christian ethics in the context of current events, discussion and debate.

We are living through one of the recurrent periods in Christian history when the word "new" gets attached to the views of certain writers and preachers who swerve from the orthodox path. So "new theology" and "new morality" are in the air again, and popular journalism is making the public aware of debates and tensions that used to be secluded within academic pamphlets or seminary walls. The average layman is aware that something is happening in the area of Church thought and practice, but he is not quite sure what it is. Some are vaguely pleased that Christianity seems to be catching up with a scientific and revolutionary world; others are, much less vaguely, apprehensive that the Church is about to surrender her distinctive positions in morals and religion. It would be foolish to ignore the storm signals that are out today, and to offer nothing but a rephrasing of conventional dogma. On the other hand we remember how rapidly "advanced" Christian views become outdated, especially when they turn out to be mere restatements of heresies discarded centuries ago. You can find sad volumes called *New Theology* or *New Morality* on second-hand bookshelves bearing dates like 1896 or 1901 — and nothing is duller than the radicalism of the day before yesterday.

Before the "new morality" of the 1960s passes into the museum among the period pieces, we should ask in what sense this expression is being used. There are at least three distinguishable uses in current speech and writing.

(1) Very commonly "new morality" means little more than a reference to the undoubted changes that have taken place in the way that people behave. Every generation notes that its successors are breaking away from the patterns and conventions hitherto respected, and is given to the complaint that "things are not what they used to be". The perennial lament of parents is that children show little respect for old-fashioned virtues and succumb to all kinds of new and subversive ideas. In a period of social revolution like the present the normal rate of change is violently accelerated, and established customs and patterns of behaviour seem to vanish overnight. In our day the effects of such factors as world war, increased mobility, urbanization, popular psychology, nuclear insecurity, space-thinking, new affluence, mass communication, and the dominance of what could be called the "secular point of view", have meant a very radical change in the habits, the values, the atmosphere, the accepted way of life in almost every traditional grouping of mankind. It is this new atmosphere, which we sense in the behaviour, conversation, assumptions, and art-forms of our contemporaries, that we are liable to label "the new morality". In this sense we simply mean to indicate what is actually happening. We are not talking about principles, or passing judgment. There *is* a new morality — if by that we express the undoubted truth that a considerable change has occurred in the behaviour, the ideals, the unwritten laws, the frontiers of the acceptable, in human society.

Sometimes this mere observance of what is new is subtly transformed into an ethical judgment. We are under the pressure of the modern pragmatism that sanctifies the fact. What is becomes what ought to be. The teenager's plea that "everyone else does it", implying that therefore it is surely right for him, has been elevated to an adult ethical principle. The Kinsey Reports on sexual behaviour, for example, were widely interpreted not just as a statistical assessment of how men and women are actually behaving but as an indication of what their behaviour probably should be. This "statistical morality" is usually unconscious but none the less immensely powerful. It is very easy to pass from an awareness of a "new morality" in the world around us to an uncritical acceptance of it as an ethical mentor and guide.

(2) There is, however, a "new morality" that is a conscious, explicit, and determined rejection of the ethical codes that have informed western civilization. The moral consensus of past generations, based on Judaeo-Christian traditions wedded to certain Greek ideals, is under attack by those who reject both its religious foundations and its concept of Man. The attack takes the form of either advocating some alternative ethical system, or of denying that any system whatever has meaning any more. In the first case "new morality" usually turns out to be some variety of hedonism, stoicism, or utilitarianism; in the second it replaces ethics with fatalism or nihilism. It is tempting to say that when it is a form of morality it is not new, and when it is new it is not morality. Literature and drama reflect this attitude in all its varieties. A great proportion of modern fiction indicates a complete abandonment of traditional ethics. (A "moral" novel is, of course, not one in which virtue wins over vice, but one in which men and women are seen in an ethical dimension. A fascinating thesis could be written on the respective moralities of two fictional heroes — Tom Jones and James Bond. The former is often uproariously and whole-heartedly immoral — and admits he has transgressed. For the latter traditional morality has just ceased to exist.) When we talk about the "new morality" we are sometimes referring to the dominant neo-paganism that has written off the Christian tradition, and advocating some totally different basis for human behaviour.

(3) The third way in which the expression is used today is the one that concerns us here — and that is the "new morality" movement within the Christian Church. It is linked in the popular mind with the "new theology" as suggesting a revolutionary change in the traditional Christian point of view. At the same time that Church people were startled to read about the word "God" becoming a matter of query and dispute, and "religion" being under attack by its professional representatives, they were made aware that the accepted guardians of Christian ethics were

13

having second thoughts about "absolute standards", and offering some surprising judgments in the area of sexual behaviour. A lively debate has been going on among the theologians on such matters as natural law, the commandments of God, the concepts of justice and of love, casuistry, freedom and discipline, guidance and decision, principles, and the distinctions between personal, social, national and international ethics. From time to time items from this debate spill over into the press, or reach a wider audience through vigorously-written paperbacks; and the impression is given that a revolution is under way whereby the Church is abandoning strongly-held positions and beginning to offer drastically new advice in the name of Christian ethics. No one is quite certain what this "new morality" stands for, but the rumour is that it is surprisingly permissive. For one person who carefully reads through the deliberations of the scholars there are a thousand who hear that a preacher has said that pre-marital chastity is not an absolute Christian rule, or that a minister has commended *Fanny Hill*. Hence the "new morality" is often interpreted as being an attempt of the Christian Church to adjust its standards to the pervading current of opinion in the modern world.

Anyone who attempts to go beyond this superficial judgment and find out what Christian thinkers are really saying may soon find himself wandering in a jungle of professional verbiage. The suspicion may even grow that the "newness" of current ethical thinking resides more in its vocabulary than its content. It is a good rule when confronted with a typical utterance of recent books on Christian ethics (including this one!) to ask oneself from time to time: Just what does that mean in plain English? For now that we have been instructed to dispense as far as possible with language that is reputed to be meaningless to modern man—sin, commandment, grace, judgment, heaven, hell, justification by faith, providence, communion—we have plunged into an ocean of polysyllabic jargon and come up dripping with terms and phrases that are considerably more confusing and obscure than the traditional terminology of the Church. The reader has now to struggle with such words as "contextual", "situational", "personalism", "existential moment", "secularization", "agapeic love", "depth-experience", "verification principle"—not to mention "meaningful structures" and "pluralistic behaviour-patterns". Behind what sometimes looks like a species of word-game being played by professionals there lies a serious attempt to grapple with the questions that our generation poses for traditional Christian ethics. But the discussion thus clothed in the current jargon of the schools and committee reports usually turns out to be some variation of the themes that have dominated Christian ethical discussion since New Testament times. And even the more startling statements that can be extracted *pour épater le bourgeois* are often reproductions of moral dilemmas familiar to the mediaeval schoolmen.

Since Christian morality first appeared on earth, for instance, the problem of when an accepted standard ought to be broken has been debated. This generation is not the first to discover that an occasion could arise when it might be more "Christian" to tell a lie than the truth. The classic instance is that of the homicidal maniac asking you if your friend whom he wants to kill is in the house with you. Similarly not a year has gone past since Pentecost without Christians being confronted by the question of breaking the commandment: "Thou shalt not kill." Many contemporary books on Christian ethics seem to be obsessed by these dilemmas — as if the one case in a million when the "law" might have to be literally broken is so much more important than the effective guidance provided by adherence to the standard. In the past these exceptional cases were dealt with unostentatiously. The Catholic referred to the experts on "casuistry" (a word that should carry no sinister meaning): the Protestant was inclined to say that, on rare occasions, we cannot do right — only the lesser of two wrongs. Today when a writer stumbles on one of these extreme instances of moral dilemma he is inclined to parade his discovery that the "Christian solution" may involve breaking a "law" as an example of some new insight being granted to this generation, and his finding may be headlined elsewhere as a typical example of the "new morality" in action.

It is only fair to say, however, that the writers who have been accorded the title of exponents of "new morality" have themselves been often anxious to disclaim any radical novelty in their approach. Most would be inclined to say that the emphasis in their ethical teaching lies in the rediscovery of the radical "newness" of the Gospel itself. They would maintain that this "newness" has continually been overlaid in Christian history by a moralism and legalism that derives from religious and cultural forces, and not from the New Testament. There can, after all, be no new Christian morality, only a *new* application to the circumstances of our day of the ethical revolution introduced by Christ himself.

When we consider again what that is we shall find ourselves at the very heart of the current debate. It is stated quite bluntly in the Prologue to the Fourth Gospel: "For the law was given by Moses, but grace and truth came by Jesus Christ" (John 1.17). At the risk of using an unfashionable word we might summarize the whole matter by saying that the heart of Christian morality is "grace". In the New Testament this stands for the foundation of the Christian life—our acceptance by God without regard to our merit or deserts. It also stands for the divine dynamic that enables us to respond to others in love rather than slavishly follow a book of rules of conduct. Grace came with Jesus Christ in that he embodied the reconciling love of God, and took upon himself the weight of human sin and guilt, offering a new freedom and ethical incentive to all who are united to him in faith. Grace came with his words of forgiveness and demonstration of true human liberty. Grace was the import of his sayings and his parables. Grace is the working out in his disciples in every age of the new life that he imparts. Throughout the New Testament the emphasis is on this gift of God and the spontaneous and grateful response of those who receive it. Christianity is never set out as a new code imposed on the world, but as a new kind of living made possible "in Christ". The idea of a moral law is not discarded but all law is seen as fulfilled in the obedience of love.

Already in the earliest days of the Church we have evidence that Christians found it hard fully to accept this grace as the one ground and supreme incentive of their new life. The impulse towards self-justification led to continual attempts to add to the Good News of God's free acceptance of the sinner for Christ's sake; some merit had to be claimed, some virtue seen as the reason for God's choice. Similarly, the temptation was strong to turn the Gospel itself into another kind of law, to codify its demands, and to elaborate a system to which believers must conform. The violence with which St. Paul wrote to the Galatian Church stemmed from his conviction that they had "fallen from grace"—which simply meant that they had lost the original spirit of the Gospel, and were making Christianity into yet another form of legalism. In every generation, and in every type of Christian Church, there has been this kind of "falling from grace", whereby a particular pattern of behaviour has been considered both obligatory and meritorious. Ask any typical discussion group to attempt to define the essence of Christianity today and surprisingly often the answers will indicate obedience to a law, even if that law be love to God and to our neighbour. Not many realize that their definitions fall entirely within the realm of Old Testament teaching, and are startled to be asked if the New Testament had nothing new to say.

The distinction between law and grace can, of course, be oversimplified. We cannot affirm that the religion of the Old Testament was simply legalism and knew nothing of the kind of personal communion indicated by "the grace of our Lord Jesus Christ". We cannot even say that non-biblical religions know nothing of this grace. Nor is it true to say that Christianity has abolished all thought of the law, or commandments of God. What we can and must say is that in Christ alone is grace seen as the sole basis of our acceptance by God, and love as the supreme and absolute moral guide and dynamic. Therefore Christian ethics can never be set out in the form of a set of rules of behaviour — not even one that puts love to God and man at the head of the list. Its starting-point must always be the new relationship to God "for Christ's sake", and its temper that of what St. Paul calls the "glorious liberty of the children of God" (Rom. 8. 21).

The simplest analogy we can use to understand this difference between law and grace is also probably nearest to the mind of Christ as expressed in the Gospels. A child brought up in an institution where the rules are fair but strict, where rewards and punishments are inexorable, and where there is a conspicuous lack of personal affection, will probably have a clear sense of right and wrong, and may (or may not) develop into what we call an upright citizen. He will certainly have a totally different attitude from that of the child who is raised in a sincere and sensible Christian home. If the first child reproduces the virtues for which we look it will be because of training in obedience, hope of reward, and fear of punishment. The same virtues in the second child will be the result of spontaneous response, unconscious imitation, natural growth within the security of love. No one will suggest that, even in the most ideal circumstances, the latter child will

17

have no need of the guidance of "laws", but it is love that is central. A reading of the Gospels leaves little doubt that Christ continually taught that we should have this kind of child-like relation to God, and that we should respond as children to a Father in gratitude and love, rather than as slaves to a master in guiltiness and fear.

This then is the "new morality" of the Gospel, and if it has never been easy to describe, it has been still more difficult consistently to practise. It has worked like leaven in what used to be called "Christendom", but it has at no time dominated any human society. It has shaped the saints of the Church and is the mark of every active Christian. It is the inspiration of Christian social action, Christian education, and Christian art. But only in our dreams has there been a society on earth so completely under the spell of Christ's new morality that the sanctions of law could disappear and the Sermon on the Mount become the normal way of life for all citizens. So Christian ethics has been concerned not only with the elucidation of what is meant by grace; it has had to deal with a host of questions arising out of the brute facts of our still sinful nature and the non-Christian, or sub-Christian environment in which we live. It is easy to say that the one Christian absolute is love, but we have to learn ever more deeply what that love really means. We have also to ask whether, in our circumstances, love does not require that there also be law. We have to decide whether Christ's new morality can be urged on those who do not accept its premise. How far, in fact, has it penetrated groups, societies, nations? What guidance does it offer in political, as opposed to personal, decisions? Does it always lead two Christians to identical answers to a pressing problem? What compromises have to be made, if any, when we deal with certain elements of our imperfect society? How do you distinguish Christian liberty from licence, and Christian discipleship from moralism? These, and a host of other questions, come to view when we take seriously the new morality of Christ.

From the beginning there have been two obvious deviations from the ethics of grace derived from the Gospel. These are *licence* on the one hand, and *legalism* on the other. Every commotion in the field of Christian ethics, including that which assails us today, arises from the tugging of these forces on the New Testament message. Clearly the doctrine of grace is open to the misinterpretation that, since God forgives, then it doesn't matter what we do, and, since love is supreme, "anything goes". Thus licence reigns, and the Gospel can be made to appear a sanction for immorality. Since there were Christians in the earliest days who began to take this road (see St. Paul in some of his remarks to the Corinthian Church), it was inevitable that in reaction others would begin to erect a system of Christian laws and regulations to protect the faithful. These easily developed into a legalism in which the new morality of Christ was forgotten, and the Gospel of grace submerged in a religious apparatus of rewards and penalties, temporal and eternal.

In the name of the ethics of grace, the apostles rebuked those who became moral nihilists. "All things are lawful for me" was probably a slogan of those who stood for ethical licence. Yes, said St. Paul, "but all things are not expedient . . . I will not be brought under the power of any" (1 Cor. 6. 12). "Live as free men," said St. Peter, "not however as though your freedom were there to provide a screen for wrong-doing . . ." (1 Pet. 2. 16, *N.E.B.*). Equally forcibly the apostles fought against the reduction of the Gospel to a religion of law. "Stand fast therefore in the liberty wherewith Christ hath made us free, and be not entangled again with the yoke of bondage" was the word to the Galatians (Gal. 5. 1). "If we love one another, God dwelleth in us, and his love is perfected in us," wrote St. John (1 John 4. 12), echoing the Gospel word: "This is my commandment, That ye love one another, as I have loved you" (John 15. 12). It was clear, right from the beginning, that the practice of the new morality of Christ was not going to be easy. It is the morality of the "new man" who lives by the Spirit, and the "old man" is always waiting in the wings.

There are undoubtedly some new factors in modern life that arouse all kinds of questions in the field of Christian ethics, and it is these that give rise to the fears — or the hopes — that a revolution is taking place. The new perspectives opened up by space exploration and the vast time-scale to which we have become accustomed have generated scepticism about the validity of any ethical system that dates from the early days of the Roman Empire. As soon as men begin to feel that there is something parochial about the morality in which they were raised, they are vulnerable to the suggestion that "everything is relative". Some such phrase is commonly used to dismiss any thought of an absolute right or wrong, and to justify the abandonment of any traditional "Thou shalt not". There is also a new bewilderment in our moral judgments caused by recent experiments and discoveries in the field of drugs, brain surgery, "hidden persuaders", and techniques of personality change. New questions arise as to the limits of experimentation with human life and conduct, and new doubts as to the freedoms of moral choice. The shrinking together of the human race, with its paradoxical corollary of a sense of alienation and estrangement, is provoking a fresh examination of accepted codes of behaviour. In general the accelerating rate of change in our human condition, and the swift emergence of new patterns of life, are bound to put a heavy strain on any morality that is rooted in the past.

It is not surprising, therefore, that from one side the cry goes up for a vigorous reaffirmation of traditional ethics, while from the other we hear a demand for radical revision. It was never more necessary to keep our heads. Those who are afraid to confront the new situation and desire above all else to be reassured that the moral standards of grandpapa are inviolable need to be reminded that true Christian morality was never a book of rules, and that the Spirit of Christ has always resisted the attempt to sanctify any particular expression of Christianity in action. The new morality of Christ implies a new response to the challenge of each new era, and a re-evaluation of priorities in the light of "Thou shalt love". On the other hand, those who would jettison the standards of the past, and talk about a "new morality" that is tailored for our age, might pause to ask whether they are responding to the Spirit of God or the climate of the times. Though Christian ethics has found varied expression through the centuries, in its genuine form it has never been simply determined by the pressures of the world. Christians are called to live *in* the world but not to be *of* the world. They should therefore be immune to the slogans "Everybody does it" "no one can possibly believe . . ." or (beloved by popular radical theologians) "unacceptable by modern man".

It is useful to remember that basic ethics deals with some constant features of human life. Readers of the Bible who are not blinkered by prejudices or enslaved by some theory have little difficulty in recognizing the moral dilemmas and ethical choices confronting its characters. They are not prevented by the alien

20

scenery and ancient ideas from identifying with the human beings whom they find there confronting God and their fellow men. An astronaut could spin through space reading the Book of Psalms or the Sermon on the Mount without feeling he was simply passing the time in archaeological research: these words would speak to him as vividly as to any nomad of the desert. The style of life inspired by the Word of God is as relevant to the world of tomorrow as to that of yesterday. Goodness, unselfishness, honesty, purity, love — these are not qualities that date. No matter how clever we become in the mastery and exploitation of the universe, no matter how far we may range into the unknown, we remain men and women with constant questions as to how we are to live together in harmony, and what resources are available for the implementing of our ideals. Ethics is not a science in the sense that new discoveries constantly outdate the findings of the past. There is no more reason to suppose that by virtue of living in the twentieth century we have nothing to learn from the first than to maintain that because we have some brilliant modern writers therefore Dante and Shakespeare can be relegated to the scrap-heap. There is no conceivable human situation "beneath the visiting moon" — or on it — where the command to love God with all our heart and our neighbour as ourself would be irrelevant.

Behind the current questioning of conventional Christian ethics there lies a fundamental question of belief. We are not engaged only in a debate about the application of New Testament morality to the conditions of modern society. Too often Christian ethics is the subject of discussion without sufficient attention to the adjective. *Christian* ethics differs from other systems of morality in resting entirely on the unique revelation of God in Jesus Christ. So powerfully is morality linked with faith in God — Father, Son, and Holy Spirit — that anything like a code of morals can hardly be extracted from the New Testament documents. Christian behaviour depends on our communion with the Father-God, our experience of the Risen Christ, our being led by the Holy Spirit. Attempts are frequently made to detach the ethics from what is called the "religion". We all know the man who says: "I'm not a religious man but I try to live by the Sermon on the Mount," or "I've no time for dogmas but I stand for the Christian way of life." This attitude sounds reasonable and its exponents are often most attractive people, but biblically and historically there is no warrant for such a divorce of religion and ethics. From the earliest days the Christian way of life (and before the word "Christianity" was used it was simply known as "the Way") was centred on the divine Lord who was the conqueror of sin and death; it was never simply an ethic deriving from the teachings of the rabbi from Nazareth. Through the years the various forms of this Way have always been informed and inspired by what is usually called religious conviction.

We cannot therefore engage in a discussion of Christian ethics today without raising the question of basic beliefs. *The* major decision in our moral debate is, in fact, whether or not our sense of right and wrong, our ideals, our motivation is related to a divine order. Rationalist and humanist ethics have, of course, steadily denied that the divine reference is relevant, useful, or even possible. Until recently Christian thinkers have affirmed the supreme importance of belief in God as the source and sustainer of our moral values. We are now experiencing a serious attempt by those who write from within the Christian Church to eliminate the transcendent, the supernatural, the "Father-image", from our theology, and therefore to suggest an ethic that can be stated in purely secular terms. The current trend has gone much farther than the familiar attack on our "images of God". The whole of Christianity is to be rethought and reformulated as a secular Gospel — though where the "Good News" comes from if there is no order beyond the secular, no God beyond what we see in man, it is hard to understand. So-called "new morality" is thus very closely dependent on "new theology", and, whether or not we are sympathetic to the efforts of the latter, we cannot discuss Christian ethics without stimulating our thinking on the subject of religious belief.

Chapter Two

THE THEOLOGY BEHIND OUR ETHICS

To the modern ear the word "ethics" has a more lively and contemporary ring than the word "theology". A newspaper headline in which "ethics" occurs will usually catch the attention; certainly if the cognate word "morals" is used the reader will be well and truly hooked, as the popular press knows only too well. Ethics, morals — these suggest immediately a report or a discussion on the vagaries of human behaviour, and what can be more interesting? Quite apart from the normal human curiosity about the eccentricities of our fellow men and their deviation from accepted standards, we are all involved in the complicated business of making decisions on the basis of what we feel to be right or wrong, and passing judgments according to our estimate of good and evil. At a time when western civilization seems to have, to a considerable degree, abandoned the traditional framework of moral judgment, the ethical debate has emerged from the philosophical schools to be vigorously waged in the home, on the street, in the club, in the pub, in newspapers, magazines, radio and television, studded with the familiar questions: "Why is it wrong?" "What is your standard?" "Who is the judge?" "What makes it good?" "How do we decide?" "Where's your authority?" and "How do you know?"

Ethics, then, is a lively and topical subject in which nearly everybody is interested. We are aware that there is hardly an item on the front page of the daily paper that raises no ethical question — crime and punishment, racial conflicts, international affairs, traffic accidents, narcotic addiction, bribery and corruption, whatever story you read carries moral implications and stimulates ethical debate. There has been a convention in politics of isolating specific questions as "moral issues" which are somehow distinguished from the other matters of controversy. In the United States these are usually injected into the election campaigns with some care as potential dynamite that could disrupt normal party affiliations. In Great Britain such "moral issues" are usually recognized by leaving them to the so-called "free vote" of the Members of Parliament. But it becomes increasingly apparent that this distinction is unreal and artificial. In what sense, in America, is an alleged gift of a television set to a member of the Administration a moral issue while the Civil Rights Act is not? And in what sense, in Britain, is the misbehaviour of a Cabinet Minister a moral issue while the Suez crisis was not? We are beginning to realize that ethical questions lie behind every serious decision in modern society, and that "morality" has a wider reference than bribery or sex.

If ethics has thus moved to the forefront of current interest and discussion, the same cannot be said about theology. The "Queen of the Sciences" was deposed very long ago, and in recent years has hovered like a poor relation round the doorways of the palace. Theology has shared the fate of metaphysics in a world where many believe that physics has the final word to speak. The popular impression is that theology deals with matters that are not only obscure but purely speculative. The old gibe about the philosopher being the man in a dark cellar looking for a black cat that isn't there, and the theologian being the man who claims he has found it, quite fairly represents a widespread suspicion. The recent eruption of theology into popular discussion with the publication of *Honest to God* scarcely amounts to a reversal of opinion, for at least some of the excitement was generated by the impression that a bishop was publicly wondering about that black cat too. It is vaguely assumed that theology has to do with finding supernatural reasons for our ethical activity, and the feeling is that we can get along nicely without them. While questions about war and peace, birth control, racial justice, and pre-marital sex are seen by all to be of the greatest practical importance, such theological questions as are, for instance, posed by the Shorter Catechism — "Are there more Gods than one?" "How many persons are there in the Godhead?" "What is effectual calling" — are apt to be considered irrelevant mystifications.

Thus the ethical injunctions of the Bible are reckoned to be detachable from its theology. Much lip-service is paid to the Sermon on the Mount on the assumption that its precepts are valid and practicable without any reference to the heavenly Father of whom its Author continually spoke, and upon whom he so obviously and confidently relied. In the same way the most popular text from the Old Testament today is the injunction of Micah to "do justly and to love mercy". We recognize that most of our ethical problems lie right in this area of justice and mercy, and their reconciliation in practice. This modern digest form of the text lops off the theology from the beginning and the end; for what Micah said was: "What doth the Lord require of thee, but to do justly, and to love mercy, and to walk humbly with thy God?" (Mic. 6. 8). The introduction is ignored as a piece of primitive mythology, and the conclusion is excised as meaningless piety.

This popular disentangling of ethics from theology has been going on throughout this century with considerable assistance from writers like Bertrand Russell and Julian Huxley, for whom religion is not only a quite unnecessary hypothesis, but a serious obstacle to the achievement of justice and mercy in human relations. They quote copiously from the seamier side of the record of organized religion, and draw attention to the many deplorable instances of religious persecution and obscurantism. It is theology, they claim, that has often sanctified conditions of flagrant injustice, opposed or ignored movements for social reform, and on questions like war, capital punishment, marriage laws and birth control has at times shown a most unmerciful attitude. In more recent years theology has been further nudged out of consideration by its association with metaphysics. Where philosophy becomes a matter of linguistic analysis it is to be expected that theological propositions will get short shrift. In popular terms that means that statements about God and the supernatural will be regarded as mere emotional noises without content. We have also to reckon with the invasion of the soul — considered by many to be the last refuge of the theologian — by the psychologist armed with a new and prestigious terminology. All in all, it is not surprising that the cry has gone up: "Let's have ethics without theology, morality without religion."

If we take theology to be, in a broad sense, a statement about the ultimate nature of things, and ethics to be a statement about the obligations of human behaviour, then the contention of theological ethics is that we *ought* to behave in a certain way because this is how things *are* in the divine Ground of our Being. As the Old Testament puts it: "Ye shall be holy: for I the Lord your God am holy" (Lev. 19. 2) and the New: "You must therefore be all goodness, just as your heavenly Father is all good" (Matt. 5. 48, *N.E.B.*). This is the basic position of a truly theological ethic—the correspondence of the imperative with the indicative. We *ought* to be like this, for ultimately this *is* how the universe is governed. It has not always been understood that this is the fundamental connection between our belief in God and our moral obligations. There are religions that make no such affirmation about the character of their God or gods. The obligation is laid on mankind as an arbitrary demand with no kind of guarantee that it has any echo in the divine Being. All sorts of commandments and taboos have been accepted as divinely imposed on men without any necessary relation to the character of their god. Even within the Christian tradition it is not uncommon to find people who seem to believe that the justice and mercy that God commands them to practise are not necessarily honoured by God himself. Theological ethics has always been haunted by the spectre of a divine Being who may turn out to be quite differently motivated than by the ethical code he instils in the human family. It is therefore important for us to realize that when we talk about the theology behind our ethics we are adhering to the biblical view that lies behind the whole Judaeo-Christian moral tradition. This affirms without qualification that the moral demand that is laid upon man is based on the nature of God himself. To express this in the most general terms, we can say that for theological ethics the central truth is that the universe itself is on the side of the goodness, the justice, the love, the integrity that we experience as moral demands on us. In simple Christian language we would say of our search for the good life: "If God be for us, who can be against us?" (Rom. 8. 31) "Blessed are they which do hunger and thirst after righteousness: for they shall be filled" (Matt. 5. 6).

This theological backing for morality has, then, very deep roots in human experience. It is difficult to discover any community where morality is entirely divorced from any religious conviction, and there is a hidden theology behind nearly all the ethical judgments that are commonly made today. The fact that in English the word "God" and the word "good" are etymologically identical is a luminous symbol of this fusion. (Incidentally, you might expect that the religious man would be inclined to exclaim "My God!" in moments of stress, and the ethical humanist would say "My goodness" — instead of the other way around!) Even those who have rejected religious belief altogether have not been able to disentangle their moral convictions from their theological basis. They may speak freely of non-theological ethics, of morality without religion, but within the structure of their ethics there is usually concealed a metaphysic — a belief about the ultimate nature and direction of the universe. The idea of a personal God may be totally rejected, but moral judgments are still made on the basis of a faith that somehow the tides of history or the laws of science are on their side. That is what I mean by a hidden theology. When the Communist makes his moral decisions, which often seem to us in callous disregard for standards we have been trained to honour, he does so on the basis of his faith that he is co-operating with the ineluctable laws of development towards the Marxist millennium. When the humanist launches his protests against the evils of our society, even when his targets are the follies and mis-demeanours of the Church, he is often borrowing from the theology he rejects. It is only from a culture permeated with Christian ideals that the eloquent moral protests of a Voltaire, a Paine, a Bertrand Russell, can arise. The strongest attacks on Christian theology and Christian practice are nearly always made in the name of moral principles derived from the Christian Gospel. The humanist can never quite shake off the ghost of his own, or his ancestors' religion.

Our task then is not to put up a last-ditch defence of theology as the basis of our ethics. Everyone who makes moral decisions does so with some faith in the ultimate validity of the principles on which he acts, unless he is either a determinist (in which case he cannot properly speak of "decisions" at all) or a naturalist for whom human behaviour is reduced to the animal level of "doing what comes naturally". What we have to examine is the *Weltanschauung* that underlies the accepted morality, whether this is explicitly formulated as a theology or not. Behind every experi-ence of the moral demand, the "ought" in our lives, is a faith in some transcendent reality, that which simply "is". I suppose this is what G. K. Chesterton had in mind when he remarked that what he wanted to know about a prospective landlady was not this or that detail about her personal habits, but her entire philosophy of life.

The specific challenge to Christian ethics comes with the questioning of the God about whom Christian theology speaks. For even those who grant that there is some kind of metaphysic behind their ethical ideals will often strongly repudiate any thought of a personal God as the source and norm of our moral life. They are satisfied that the God spoken of in the Bible and the creeds of the Church is a mere projection of the human conscience, a Father-figure that was a natural and useful symbol of objective morality during the childhood of the race, just as he is during the childhood of each individual. At a primitive stage, it is argued, we need the crutch provided by the image of this Father-God, the one who lays down the law and rewards or punishes according to our deserts. But the time comes for each one of us, and has now come for the entire race, to be free from any such fantasy-figure, who should henceforth be relegated to the limbo of fairies, hobgoblins, and Santa Claus. Any theology, therefore, that still speaks of such a God — no matter how sophisticated its approach — cannot be taken seriously by modern man. The crutch must be resolutely thrown away and not reintroduced in any new disguise. If the starting-point of Christian ethics is, as I believe: "Glory be to the Father, and to the Son, and to the Holy Spirit," then we must meet the challenge of modern atheism head-on.

This does not mean that the Christian is unable to sympathize with his contemporary, to whom the thought of a living God is obscure to the point of impossibility, and for whom the idea of being responsible to any kind of personal divinity is utterly archaic. Every intelligent believer has struggled with the problem of expressing his apprehension of a God who cannot be just *a* God without ceasing to be God, one who is personal without the limitations that word normally implies, one who is not identical with the universe and yet cannot be separated from it, one who cannot be called *a* Being without suggesting that other beings exist independently of him, but for whom Being itself seems too vague and impersonal a name. To say that over the centuries the average Christian has simply passed from a concrete image of a Person "up there" to a slightly vaguer but equally crude image of a Person "out there" is not only a caricature of the beliefs of the

Christian today but also a travesty of the views of the compilers of the ancient creeds. The Christian who has wrestled in every age with the question of God's immanence and transcendence, who feels the need of symbols to express what cannot be expressed in propositions, who has known what it is to say with Job: "Oh that I knew where I might find him!" (Job 23. 3) finds himself today in a world where the threat of "God-emptiness" is at times stronger than ever. He knows what his unbelieving brothers are experiencing without having to repudiate the historic language of belief. In order to express his solidarity with his atheist contemporaries he is not compelled to translate "I believe in God the Father Almighty" into "I share with you an ultimate concern."

The Christian ethic derives from a positive belief in the living, active, personal God, known to us as "Father, Son, and Holy Spirit". The classical language of Christian theology may not be immediately understandable to the average man — and it never was. The doctrine of the Trinity may not be the best and final expression of what the Christian means by "God", but it has stood the test of time and outlasted all its rivals, even those that are being revived in modern dress. The "treasures" of the faith do indeed come to us in "earthen vessels", but a renewed understanding of the treasure is not likely to come through an indiscriminate smashing of the vessels. Since Christian ethics flows from a quite specific theology, a unique conviction about the nature and purpose of God, it might be better to re-explore the meaning of the historic symbols of the faith.

Trinity means that God is alive and personal. The doctrine is a way of saying that at the heart of all things is One in whom all that we value as personal — goodness, love, justice, truth, community — is for ever alive. Only thus can the Christian most adequately speak about the God he has come to know — a God who is not less but more alive than we are, a God who is not less but more personal than we are, a God who is not bare unity but reflects in his nature the values of community. Just as it is easy to caricature the belief in the Heavenly Father as an image of an old man sitting on a cloud out there, so it is easy to dismiss the doctrine of the Trinity as a cross between a mathematical equation and a celestial committee-meeting. There is nothing new about the discovery that Christian doctrines lend themselves to distortion by both believers and unbelievers. Provided we remember the limitations of language, and the power of symbol, we shall find it hard to dismiss the historic creeds of the Church. Without the trinitarian belief that has inspired the Church, Catholic and Reformed, for two thousand years, the Christian ethic would surely have been vastly different in content and in power. For a living, personal ethic flows from a living, personal God.

The answer to the secular atheism of today is not to be found in a Christian atheism that dissolves every vestige of the traditional image of God to leave us with an "existential encounter" with the Christ of the Gospels in the context of our relationships with our fellow men. Nor can an adequate Christian ethic be constructed on the basis of a theology that has surrendered the concept of a living, personal God to whom we are responsible, the God of the prophets and apostles. The supremacy of love — the *Agape* of the New Testament — is rooted in the belief that comes to its climax with the statement that "God is love". The apostle would not, and could not, reverse the order and say that "love is God" (1 John 4. 16) which is implied in some current attempts to restate the faith. The foundation is the eternal love of a living, personal God who seeks and finds communion with the men and women of his creation. "We love him," says the apostle, "because he first loved us" (1 John 4. 19).

The doctrine of the Trinity not only conserves for us the biblical disclosure of a living God who is both all-sufficient and self-revealing; it also offers a way of understanding the central motives of the Christian ethic. What follows is not an attempt to explicate the doctrine of the Trinity or to make an artificial bridge between classical statements of the faith and the data of our moral life. It is rather an examination of the keynotes of Christian ethics in the light of the revelation of God from which they are derived.

What is it that makes Christian ethics specifically Christian? That is a question that needs to be answered, for a great deal that goes under the phrase "Christian way of life" today can hardly be distinguished from the ethical ideals of humanism, Judaism, or many other movements that make no profession of Christian faith. And it is obvious to a student of the New Testament that a great many ethical precepts commended there are shared by other non-Christian strands in our western tradition. There is no need to deplore or to minimize the area of moral ideal that is shared by Christians with those of other faiths or of none. The days are surely gone when the words that literally denote a denial of Christian belief—"miscreant", "infidel", "heathen"—can be hurled around as terms of abuse, as if the man who denies the divinity of Jesus Christ will be likely to steal my coffee-spoons or assault my wife. But the question still remains: What makes Christian ethics Christian? There must be some unique factor in the approach of the believing Christian to the good life and the moral decisions in which we are all involved.

For that unique factor there is a unique word, a word that it has not been possible to replace or eliminate in the modern Christian vocabulary. That word is *grace*. The starting-point of Christian ethics is not the acceptance of a new law of life introduced by Jesus Christ, but of a new status and a new power offered and conferred by him. Grace is the New Testament word used to describe the action of God in Christ whereby we are accepted by him just as we are, with all our vices and imperfections, and given a new nature with the impetus to fulfil God's will. At the heart of the Christian ethic lies the prayer of the Publican in the parable: "God be merciful to me a sinner" (Luke 18. 13) and the confession of St. Paul: "I can do all things in him who strengthens me" (Phil. 4. 13, *R.S.V.*).

Christians share with all who are morally serious the effort to "do justly, and to love mercy, and to walk humbly with thy God". But they start from the premise that we need to be forgiven for our utter failure, a failure that is not to be measured over against the greater or lesser failures of our fellow men but over against the perfection that we see in Christ. Virtue then is not seen as an achievement of which we can be proud but as a gift that comes with the forgiveness of God. This is what accounts for the paradox that those who have been accounted the greatest saints have usually been most acutely conscious of their sins. Even allowing for a degree of morbid introspection, and admitting that an over-emphasis on sin has sometimes paralysed the ethical action of the Church, we are conscious that grace has been the factor for making humility central in the Christian ethic. The absolute ethic of Christ with its demands for a total, inward, and inclusive purity, honesty and love forbid the Christian the luxury of self-satisfaction and final achievement, while the realization of moral progress is attributable to God alone. "Work out your own salvation," says St. Paul, adding at once, "for it is God which worketh in you" (Phil. 2. 12, 13).

The morality of grace is unique in its motive and its dynamic. Religion has often worked upon morality with the carrot and stick: "Do good so that God will love you" "Don't do evil or you'll go to hell." It has thus often added to the burden of the sincere man or woman, expanding enormously the area of bad conscience and suggesting an infinite number of ways in which we have to strive to justify ourselves before God. When Jesus said: "Come unto me, all ye that labour and are heavy laden, and I will give you rest" (Matt. 11. 28) it was this crushing effect of religion he almost certainly had in mind. For the grace he represented meant that morality was no longer to be a burdensome obligation with which we stagger towards heaven, but a spontaneous and grateful response to the mercy and forgiveness of God. The motive behind the Christian ethic is, then, gratitude for what God has done, not an effort to win his favour by our goodness. And the dynamic for the good life is not discovered in our ability to observe more and more rules of conduct, but in the communicated strength of the One who has lived for us, died for us, and risen from the dead to be the Deliverer and Companion on our way.

The grace of our Lord Jesus Christ is thus the theological centre from which our Christian ethic comes. This is where the Triune God meets us — in the coming of the Son. Grace is not some mysterious quality of God kept in some heavenly reservoir and channelled to us through ecclesiastical pipe-lines. Grace is personal. Grace is Christ meeting us at the point of our greatest need. Grace is freedom: freedom from the burden of sin, freedom from the bondage of both religion and irreligion, freedom from the need for self-justification, freedom from the fears that haunt our moral decisions. Christian ethics is thus something very different from a new and stringent code imposed on top of the Old Testament Law. A superficial reading of the Sermon on the Mount with its reiteration, amplification and extension of the Ten Commandments, and its insistent question "What do ye more than others?" (Matt. 5. 47), might lead us to conclude that Christian ethics is nothing else than the demand for perfection. In the context of the entire life and teaching of Jesus, and the insights of the apostolic Church, however, we see that the essence of the new life is not law but grace. The perfection is not imposed as an impossible ideal but as already present in Christ intó whose Kingdom we come, not as moral princes who are qualified to enter, but as beggars who have nothing to offer but our need. Within that Kingdom we live by grace, which means that we are responding to the personal presence of the King in gratitude and love rather than striving to climb the endless ladder of his laws. We know the difference between a child brought up in a strict institution where he is forced to obey a set of rules, and a child reared in a home full of Christian love. For the one it is: "Be good, or . . ."; the other can experience a natural and spontaneous moral development in happy response to what he receives. At the heart of Christian ethics is the grace that means growth in the Father's home. "In this was manifested the love of God toward us, because that God sent his only begotten Son into the world, that we might live through him" (1 John 4. 9).

But what about this love of God? If the grace of our Lord Jesus Christ is our personal contact with the Triune God, what are we to say about the doctrine of the "Father Almighty, Maker of heaven and earth"? In what way does the theological conviction of the Creator-God impinge upon our ethical behaviour?

This is where we come up against the traditional Christian teaching about our responsibility to, and dependence upon, the eternal God from whom we come and to whom we go. If Christian ethics is centred upon grace, it is also true that this cannot be isolated from the ideas of responsibility and dependence. The God whom we meet in Jesus Christ as grace, is also the sovereign God to whom we are answerable and upon whom we utterly depend. There has therefore always been at the centre of Christian ethics a sense of reverence and trust. The personal presence of the Father Almighty, Maker of heaven and earth, has, as it were, provided the supernatural context of our natural decisions.

It is this doctrine of the presence of the Creator-God that is exposed to criticism and attack in our generation. There are those who feel that while modern man can still find in Jesus Christ a grace and freedom that gives meaning to their lives, it is impossible for us to think in any real sense of a God who is actually in charge of our world, whose presence we can know and on whose will we are dependent. We have learned, of course, that God must not be sought only at the extremities of our life, in the moments of crisis and despair. We have learned also the folly of looking for him to fill the gaps in our knowledge of the world we live in. But now we are told that, since man has come of age, we must cease looking for him at all, and live "as though God did not exist". This radical restatement of the Christian attitude is perhaps a necessary reaction to crude popular notions of the "Man Upstairs" and the unfortunate habit of referring to natural disasters as "acts of God". It is also a repudiation of the pious evasion of responsibility that is the characteristic of some of our prayers, and a summons to accept the full and dangerous freedom that has been committed to us. But the impact of the biblical revelation is surely as strong today as at any time in the past. For the Creator-God of the prophets and apostles is no *deus ex machina* who can be politely ushered out of his universe by man, no matter how grown-up he may have come to be. Nor is he a kind of superstitious explanation of various queer goings-on in the recesses of the universe. He is not the temporary explanation of what we cannot yet understand; he is the only explanation of why there is anything at all. He is not the meaning of this and that in our experience, but of everything that is. And he is the author of that freedom which is our glory and our doom.

Something is removed from the Christian ethic the moment we cease to believe in the presence of the Creator-God to whom we are responsible and upon whom we depend. It may be necessary to guard ourselves against language that suggests false thoughts of God, like those stickers that advertise the desire of the car-owner to "keep God in America", or those speeches that are for ever taking him in or out of our public schools. We may often have evaded our moral duties in society, or resisted the advance of scientific investigation, in the name of a false reverence and reliance upon God. But depending on God in the wrong way cannot be corrected by not depending on him at all. Who can read the Gospels without an immense impression of the steady, day-by-day, hour-by-hour reliance of Jesus on his heavenly Father? And is there one single factor about our modern existence, with all its vast extension of knowledge about nature and ourselves, that warrants the conclusion that such a reliance is impossible for us?

Christian ethics will not recover the full sense of personal responsibility until we restore the theological emphasis on the personal presence of the Father-God; will not recover a sense of reverence for all creation until we are theologically assured of the reality of the Creator-God; will not be animated by a faith that removes the mountains of social evil around us until we learn again what it means to say: "I believe in God the Father Almighty, Maker of heaven and earth."

We have considered the ethical power of the doctrines of grace and of the Creator-Presence. But there is still one more link between the moral life of the Christian and the Triune God in whom he believes. So far we have been speaking of ethics and theology as if our concern were only with the individual — how you and I behave, and what you and I believe. But we cannot be isolated as though each person was enclosed in his responsibilities and related to his God in independence of his fellows. We are born into a family and live in a community. Our personality emerges as we are related to one another in the traffic of every day. And from the beginning a sense of community has been a strong mark of the Christian ethic.

An examination of the New Testament will reveal what our modern individualism has so often forgotten — that the Christian way of life is a community-way, a communion, a fellowship of mutual support. That is most strikingly apparent in the account of the first days of the Church. "The multitude of them that believed were of one heart and of one soul: neither said any of them that ought of the things which he possessed was his own; but they had all things common" (Acts 4. 32). Christian ethics, then, was not launched as a new philosophy attached to the name of a divine Teacher. It emerged in the practice, the common life, of a group of men and women whose behaviour earned them the title of "the Way". The pagan world knew that a new ethical power was abroad not when they read a copy of the Sermon on the Mount, but when they saw a Christian Church and said: "See how these Christians love one another."

We cannot understand the imperatives of the New Testament aside from the context of the Church. It was only within this communion that the full realization of this new ethic was possible. That is why we run into trouble whenever we take any specific precept of the New Testament and try to make it the basis for

35

legislation in the world. That is why we find the emphasis – often so disturbing to us – on love for "the brethren", as if the outside world was not to be loved in quite the same way. There was, of course, always a danger of the wrong kind of double standard appearing; and Christian ethics has often suffered from a tendency to ingrowing charity. But basically the stress on the "brotherhood" arose from the experience that only in the fellowship of the Spirit could the powers of the new ethic be fully realized. In the deepest sense of the phrase, they needed one another. They were "members one of another" (Eph. 4. 25) for they were integrated into the Body of Christ.

It is surely abundantly clear that this social context of Christian ethics, this sense of oneness in Christ, this realization of the new ethical power as a communal gift, derives directly from the revelation of the Triune God as Holy Spirit. The "fellowship of the Holy Spirit" was not a vague theological formula invented by St. Paul to impress first-century mystics and philosophers. It was the Christians' way of referring to the immediate, awe-inspiring, supernatural realization of the presence of God as the living bond of their unity and inward strength of the new community in Christ. The Pentecost experience is decisive for the Christian Church. The grace of Christ was with them as they knew themselves to be personally called by him. The presence of the Father-God was with them as they waited on him in humble trust and prayer. And then the Holy Spirit was with them to unite them in the certainty of their faith and empower them as a new community of love. Trinity was not for them at that moment a theological doctrine to be elaborated in words. Trinity was God with them, God for them, God in them – creating the new community that was the Church. The ethics, the way of life, on which they embarked was not a series of individual experiments on the part of Peter, James, John and the others. It was an adventure in which they engaged as a group of men and women who had discovered God's design for his human family.

There is, then, no understanding of Christian ethics without a grasp of the theology from which it rose. If the marks of the Christian way are a thankful and spontaneous love based on the grace that reaches us in Christ, a reverence for and trust in the Father-God, and a surrounding and supporting community of the Spirit, then we can see why the theology is the source and inspiration of the ethic. We do not face the task of Christian living by confronting a stern and daunting ethical code, or by counting our moral assets, or even by summoning up an inward strength. We begin by saying: "Glory be to the Father, and to the Son, and to the Holy Spirit; as it was in the beginning, is now, and ever shall be, world without end, Amen."

Chapter Three

THE ENCOUNTER
BEHIND OUR THEOLOGY

IN our thinking about ethics it is important to perceive what implicit or explicit theology lies behind our judgments. We have seen that nearly all the ethical convictions by which men have lived have been based on some affirmation about the ultimate nature of life itself and the universe that we inhabit. The Christian way of life, in particular, derives from the Christian belief that we have to do with a sovereign God who meets us as Father, Son, and Holy Spirit. This marriage of ethics and theology is witnessed to throughout the Bible. The Ten Commandments are prefaced by the words: "I am the Lord thy God, which have brought thee out of the land of Egypt, out of the house of bondage" (Exod. 20. 2). Thus, before we are told what we ought to do, we are, as it were, briefed on the situation in which we act. This is our God: therefore this is how we must behave. In the New Testament the Son of God declares: "As I have loved you, so you are to love one another" (John 13. 34, *N.E.B.*). The Gospel declaration of God's love for us in Christ is thus the basis of the great commandment of human love. St. Paul's epistles are the clearest reflection of this ethical-theological union. The moral imperatives which the apostle regularly fired at the Churches he had founded were always the outcome of his theological affirmations. You will normally find his ethical imperatives in the last chapters of his letters, preceded by solid indicatives about God and his action for us in Christ. The imperative: "Be ye reconciled" for instance, follows the indicative that "God was in Christ, reconciling the world unto himself" (2 Cor. 5. 19, 20).

It would, however, be a great mistake to imagine that when we have celebrated the marriage of ethics and theology we have solved the problem of the impact of our Christian faith on modern life. For ethics is, above all else, a practical subject. It has to do with our daily behaviour—what we are thinking, what we are doing, how we treat other people, and the kind of person we are. Ethical theory is merely a reflection upon our human life, an attempt to understand and to give intellectual coherence to the motives and impulses that make us what we are. It is a necessary task but it is conducted in the chambers of the mind and not in the traffic of the street. Moral philosophy is thus a mental exercise that may, or may not, have any impact on our daily life. It would be naïve to suppose that an exclusive community of moral philosophers sealed off from the world in some kind of ethical monastery would be a kind of heaven on earth. (It would probably be nearer hell.) It is quite possible to be a brilliant student of ethics and a most unpleasant person. In the same way theology is an intellectual reflexion upon the things we claim to believe. It is an attempt to understand and give coherence to the statements of faith. It is conducted in words and mental concepts. The vehicles of theology are dialogue and debate. It is always at least once removed from our religious life. Therefore it is only fair to add that an exclusive community of Christian theologians would not necessarily sparkle with all the Christian virtues. (For any with experience of the *odium theologicum* in full flight this will seem an understatement.)

When we are considering the impact of Christian people in our world, and asking ourselves what sort of influence is, or can be, exerted by Christians in the practical affairs of today — personal, community, national, international and universal — there is something even more important than the theology behind our ethics. And that is the religion behind our theology. By religion I mean our actual encounter with God, our prayers, our sense of his presence, our experience of his guidance, our conversion to Christ, our realization of his Spirit, our worship, and what we might call "the impulses of grace" in our human relationships and enjoyment of the world and the arts. Most of us are aware of what is meant by "religion" in this sense, however hard it is to define. It is our practical response to the truth that theology seeks to elaborate. It means the operative beliefs of a man or woman, their total response to the revelation of God. It is hard to resist unfashionable terminology and say that it is the dimension of the supernatural in their lives. It is hard to define in words precisely because it is not theology, but the raw material out of which theology comes. And theology can never do more than approximate to what religion means, since there is an element in our encounter with God that passes beyond what can be expressed in concepts and in words.

There is currently a powerful objection in some quarters to this conception of religion, the supernatural, and all that used to be known as piety. Bonhoeffer's phrase "religionless Christianity" has been plucked from its context and used as a slogan for an indiscriminate attack on all traditional expressions of what the Church has known as "the spiritual life". A mood of impatience with the pattern of piety associated with organized churches has led to explosions like this from Monica Furlong: "I am deeply involved in formal religion myself, owe it an overwhelming debt, and am only brash enough to scoff at it ninety per cent of the time. But for those who have ears to hear and lips to tell, it is common knowledge that the foundations have shivered, that there are cracks a mile wide in its walls, that the hot ashes are falling like rain upon our piety, and that the lava is curling about our sacred objects. When we try to walk in the old paths of religion we find them broken and obliterated." This is only one of thousands of diatribes against the faith of our fathers as it is represented by the word "religion" in today's vocabulary. The impression is given that this religion is on its way out to the accompaniment not only of the scorn of the sceptic but the cheers of enlightened Christians.

What lies behind this attempt to abandon the notion of a specific religious dimension? Why do we hesitate to speak any more of the "spiritual life"? Why has "piety" become a dirty word and "supernaturalism" a term of abuse?

There are at least three strong reasons for questioning the traditional use of these expressions and repudiating the picture of the Christian life they have instilled.

(1) First, it must be admitted that the use of the word religion to refer to a certain limited number of thoughts and activities has tended to foster the notion that our encounter with God takes place in a special area of our lives that is isolated from the traffic of every day. The words "sacred" and "secular", in popular thinking, encourage us to think of a dichotomy between our normal concerns as a citizen — our homes, our work, our recreations, our politics, our social interests — and our religious activities, such as prayer, worship, evangelism, and the reading of the Bible.

Hence we often hear remarks like: "Let the Church stick to religion and not get mixed up in secular affairs" or "I don't let my religion interfere with my business" or "A man's religion has nothing to do with his fitness to be President of the United States" or "I've nothing against modern art but don't let's have it in church". Those who speak of a "religionless Christianity" correctly point out that the Bible makes no such distinction between the sacred and the secular. Both the Old and New Testaments are full of matters we normally consider secular — loves, feuds, wars, health and welfare, domestic and foreign policies, adventures, human interest stories, the handling of money, farming, diplomacy, to mention only a few — and they contain surprisingly little of what we normally call religion. For the Bible the whole of life is claimed for God, and the prophets, the apostles and Christ himself vehemently attack the kind of religious observances that ignore plain duties in the secular world. It is Christ's insistence on relating the whole of life to the will of the heavenly Father that has led to the statement that what he did was to abolish religion.

(2) Secondly, the notion of "religion" seems to many to encourage a false picture of the world we live in. We have tended to think of life in two layers: there is the natural world whose workings are gradually explained to us by the advance of science, and where everything happens according to a law of cause and effect; and there is, above, the supernatural — a world where anything can happen. Anything that we do not understand can then be referred to this supernatural world, and from time to time an invasion of the supernatural produces what we call a miracle on earth. Religion is then confined to our dealings with this supernatural world. The difficulty with this idea is that, for the average man, it has made religion less and less relevant to modern life. For as the area of scientific competence expands, the necessity for invoking God as an explanation of the mysterious shrinks. Nothing, it seems, is now excluded from the investigation and explication of the human brain. Kant's "two things" that "fill the mind with ever-increasing wonderment and awe ... the starry heavens above ... and the moral law within" are now the territory of astrophysics and psychiatry in the popular mind. As the apparent area of the supernatural shrinks so does the incidence of miracle for the modern mind. Thus religion becomes more and more identified with superstition for many of our contemporaries

—"superstition" in its literal sense of that which "stands on top" of our normal understanding of things; in other words, an unnecessary complication.

(3) Thirdly, religion is suffering from its identification with the structure of the organized Churches. The man or woman who is sensitive to the immense needs, dangers and opportunities presented to this second half of the twentieth century may very well see religion as a vast network of ceremonies, councils, committees, rituals, traditions, and officials, none of which has much relevance to the major questions of the hour. From this point of view religion is a complicated system of beliefs and practices designed to produce and maintain a relationship to a God who is not otherwise very evident in our world. There have always been theologians who have strongly maintained that Christianity is not a religion, since the essence of the Gospel is that we cannot work our way to God up the ladder of religious observances but must simply receive him as he comes to us in Christ. But for the average man Christianity is very naturally included among the systems designed to "work the oracle" and harness God to our needs.

These are some of the reasons that lead many modern Christian writers and thinkers to deny that there is anything called religion which ought to operate upon our moral decisions. We may heed their warnings but need not accept their conclusions. Behind the sophistication of theologians and moralists there is still a stubborn conviction in the Church that there is such a thing as an encounter with God, a communion with God, a dimension of the eternal in our daily life, that cannot be simply identified with the instincts and experiences of those for whom God does not exist. And this conviction is not a mere relic of the piety of the past: it is solidly founded on the facts of the Christian life as declared in the Bible and experienced in the Church and in the world.

We may agree that the distinction between sacred and secular is ultimately false, that there is no private area to be fenced off with the notice: "Religion! Keep out!" We may agree that great damage is done by a false isolation of religion from secular affairs and from the enterprise of the arts. But there are distinctly two ways of overcoming the dichotomy. One is to be so overwhelmingly conscious of the sovereign God that we cannot abstract any human activity from his concern. The other is so to weaken or eliminate the image of God in our hearts and minds that ultimately nothing is holy. To put it simply, we may believe that there is no dichotomy because everything is sacred, or, alternatively, because everything is secular. The danger of pursuing the path of "religion-less Christianity" as an intellectual exercise, without the backing of the profound faith of a Bonhoeffer, is that it can end in a world where we live not just "as if" God did not exist, but where in fact, for us, he has vanished like the smile of the Cheshire cat (to which Julian Huxley has likened what he calls the "faint trace of God" that still hangs around). The truth is that, in order to claim the whole creation and all our activities as God's sacred trust to us, we need not less devotion, prayer, worship, concentration on the supernatural, but far more. What we mean by religion, by the encounter with God, is not an escape from the real world; it must be to some extent a withdrawal, but a withdrawal in the sense of *reculer pour mieux sauter*. We do not celebrate a mother's birthday in order to ignore her completely for the other 364 days of the year. It is a momentary concentration of a love that is thus strengthened and perpetuated. The activities involved in our encounter and communion with God are not a substitute for the practice of our faith in the home, the office, the street, the polling-booth and the market-place, but the means whereby it is kept vigorous and alive.

We may agree that there is a false way of conceiving of the natural and supernatural. It is entirely unbiblical to search for evidence of God in the gaps of scientific understanding. He is either the explanation of everything, or of nothing. And miracle is certainly not conceived by instructed Christians in terms of the occasional invasion of the natural world by the powers of the world "upstairs". But whether we like to use the word "supernatural" or not, we must confess that the Christian faith maintains that the natural world is not a self-enclosed system entirely comprehended by the instruments of science, but is dependent on, penetrated by, and ultimately absorbed into, a still more real and comprehensive world that we may call the spiritual, the supernatural, the world of God, the eternal, heaven — or any other verbal symbol that conveys this truth. To eliminate any such conception from our theology is to depart entirely from the witness of the Bible and the Church, and to divorce Christian ethics from the vital encounter with God from which it derives its content and its power. If superstition is to be defined as an "unnecessary belief" we must protest that an acknowledgment of the reality of the supernatural, in the sense of the mystery beyond and within the natural, remains for the Christian a fundamental necessity.

Again, we may agree that religion has its aspect of organizational irrelevance. Christianity often appears in the world as a great Moloch of religious machinery. It takes a Luther, a Kierkegaard, a Bonhoeffer to remind us of the God whom our "churchianity" has so often obscured. But we do not need too many little Kierkegaards to come yapping around the religious life of our churches today. The revolt against organized religion, as we know it, has now gone so far that our more radical theologians and moralists fall over each other in denouncing the piety of the man-in-the-pew. In the fashionable exercise of leaning over backwards to be as irreligious as the secular world, more than one has lost his balance. A healthy reaction from the organized pieties of the conventional Church has led to a kind of phariseeism-in-reverse that could be called the cult of "unholier-than-thou". It may well be that a great draught of fresh air is needed through the whole apparatus of our churchly activities, but God forbid that it should sweep away the essential piety that our fathers practised, the nurture of the encounter and communion with God.

The so-called "secular world" is our world too. The Christian does not stand apart as its critic and its judge. We are in it, as our Lord indicated, but not "of it". And not being "of it" implies this encounter and communion with God. It is the real religion behind our professed theology that will enable the Christian to fulfil the manifest destiny of being the salt and light of the world. The salt must not lose its savour. The light must not be hidden under the meal-tub. The world does not expect to be told that the atheist and the Christian are really saying the same thing, and that their moral judgments are virtually identical. Nor does the world understand the subtleties of an overintellectualized ethic. It looks for the instinctive Christian behaviour that flows from a genuine commitment of the soul. This is why there is a healthy scepticism abroad about some of the expressions of the "new morality" by theologians today. *Time* magazine recently quoted the following definition of the Christian obligation by a modern theologian: "There is only one thing which is always good regardless of circumstances, and that is neighborly concern, social responsibility, *agape* . . . In the situational approach of the new morality one enters into every decision-making moment armed with all the wisdom of the culture, but prepared in one's freedom to suspend and violate any rule except that one must as responsibly as possible seek the good of one's neighbor." *Time*'s comment: "quite a long thought for an eighteen-year-old during a passionate moment in the back seat of a car!"

There is no call to scoff at the attempts of our theologians to think through the formulations of Christian morality. We have seen how important it is to elucidate the theology behind our ethics. But perhaps it is time to emphasize again the religion that lies behind the theology, the actual living faith in God, the real commitment to Christ, which must always be the mainspring of Christian behaviour. Our way of life is not really controlled by certain abstract propositions that we hold about the nature of the universe, but by our actual response to the God in whom we believe. It is surely time to say out loud that, in spite of all our confusions and hesitations, Christian morality is the outcome of a personal commitment to Christ, a dependence upon God in prayer, and our experience of the worship and communion of the Church. There is no more tragic division in the Church today than that between those who profess a piety that is sealed off from living contact with the real issues of the day and those who renounce all piety in the name of involvement and social action. What is needed is the nourishment of an inner devotion that will sustain and fortify our impact on all areas of modern life. This is surely what is meant by the phrase in the Collect: "Increase in us true religion."

"I am the vine, and you the branches. He who dwells in me, as I dwell in him, bears much fruit; for apart from me you can do nothing" (John 15. 5, *N.E.B.*). These words lead us into the heart of the matter. Our behaviour as Christians, the kind of people we are, depends entirely on our relationship to Christ. What theology calls "the grace of our Lord Jesus Christ" means just this — our acceptance by Christ and our remodelling in his image. The Gospel does not just add an extra dimension to the moral obligations accepted by our society: it offers a new life, with a new centre, new motives and new power. Christian morality is then not the result of straining to live by a strict and lofty code, but the fruit of a life that is, as the New Testament says, "engrafted into Christ". "The grace of our Lord Jesus Christ" implies a reorientation of the natural life that is self-centred and self-concerned. And the reception of that grace is described with such words as "repentance", "conversion", "new birth", or "new being".

It is unfortunate that talk of conversion and rebirth is so often associated with one particular understanding of the Gospel, and one particular method of evangelism. It is doubly unfortunate when that turns out to be quite often a narrow, individualistic, self-centred type of piety that is content to ignore the social implications of the Gospel so long as "When the roll is called up yonder, I'll be there." It is, of course, entirely wrong to brand all mass evangelism in this way; but there has been a tendency in the past century for the summons to decision and conversion to be given in the context of a strangely limited theology and an arbitrarily imposed list of ethical taboos. The fact is that every part of historic Christendom has recognized that the Gospel calls for acceptance and decision. The New Testament makes the plainest plea for a "turning-round", a conversion from a life where self is God to a life where Christ is God. Nothing is said about the pattern which such a change must follow: the emphasis is on the fact and the continuing process. The question that emerges from its pages is not: "When was I converted?" or "How was I converted?" but "Am I converted? Am I at the moment facing in the right direction? Am I united with Christ?"

Briefly it can be said that Christians have described this fundamental experience in two different ways. The historic churches with what might be called "Catholic" roots tend to emphasize this commitment in terms of infant baptism, training in the faith, and constant nurture in the teaching, the worship and the sacramental actions of the Church. The Churches and sects that are associated with evangelical revivals at different periods in ecclesiastical history tend to minimize the place of the sacraments and the corporate life of the Church and to lay stress upon the necessity of definite personal decision. It is important to note that both streams of the Church's life accept the fact that a new life must be implanted, and that hence Christian morals flow from our union with Jesus Christ. Ecumenical dialogue is now revealing that there is a much less clear-cut distinction between these emphases than we used to suppose. Churches like the Anglican,

Lutheran, and Presbyterian have always managed to retain elements of both ways of regarding and fostering the new life in Christ.

What matters most for Christian ethics is the recognition that the grace of Christ is present in the world, that it must be received to be experienced as a power in our lives, and that our moral life means nothing less than growth into his image. The modern world, with its millions of sceptics, agnostics and bewildered people has to be confronted with this grace in such a way that it has meaning in the context of our society. In a missionary situation — which is to be found nearly everywhere today — conversion and adult baptism will mark the beginning of the new life. For others the stress will be upon their infant baptism, their nurture in the faith, and a challenge not to lapse from the new life into which they have been engrafted. Before we talk about "new morality" we must be sure that we are not losing the old Gospel that has sprung to life in every Christian generation. We have to disentangle this Gospel from many theological and ethical conventions that have been attached to it in recent centuries, so that we may face the new questions of our age unimpeded and unafraid. But at the centre of Christian ethics remains the living Christ, and his word is still true: "apart from me you can do nothing."

The encounter with God that is implied in the new birth is, of course, sustained in prayer. When the apostle says: "Keep yourselves in the love of God" (Jude 21) he certainly has prayer in mind. When we are told that "religion" must be scrapped, when piety is held up to scorn, we may well wonder what is happening to the activity we knew as prayer. For in blunt speech to pray is to be religious: prayer is piety. It is, in one sense, a quite frank withdrawal from the world. "When you pray," said Jesus, "go into a room by yourself, shut the door, and pray to your Father who is there in the secret place" (Matt. 6. 6, *N.E.B.*). Since we know that our Lord believed that what went on in the "secret place" would have a profound effect on our life outside, it is astonishing that the discussion of Christian ethics can go on so often and so vigorously without a mention of prayer.

If ethics is concerned both with what we are and what we do, then prayer is clearly of decisive influence. For it is the way in which we maintain that communion with God and that union with Christ which are the secret of Christian character and action. No matter how deeply we are involved in the world, no matter how thoroughly we integrate the sacred and the secular, prayer must surely always mean those moments when we cease to do anything else but commune with God. That can happen at any time and in any place. The essential is that it should happen at *some* time, and in *some* place.

It may be that we need a revolution in our thinking about the practice of prayer today. The new theologians are certainly right when they confess on our behalf that we have been depending on inherited patterns of prayer that are often meaningless and arid to us today. They are probably right when they say that our prayers are too full of words that have lost their content and their power. They are certainly not right when they encourage us to listen to the whispers of the natural man within us to the effect that *laborare est orare* and therefore all honest confrontation with our world is really prayer. The plain witness of the Bible, the centuries-long experience of the Church, and — above all — the teaching and example of Christ himself are a unanimous testimony to the necessity of private prayer for the nurture of the Christian life. It is private in its practice, but it is public in its range and its effects. "Your Father who sees what is secret will reward you" (Matt. 6. 6, *N.E.B.*). Such reward is not, of course, a prize for good conduct. The reward of praying for patience may be the arrival of the most irritating person you know. The reward of praying for purity may be a whopping temptation. The reward of praying for racial justice may be an invitation to a picket-line. The reward of praying for a friend who is ill may be a long journey to the hospital.

Prayer, as Jesus taught it, is certainly not an escape from responsibilities. It is rather the way in which we can realize the new life in Christ, the means of our constant communion with God. Instead of thinking that we have exhausted the meaning of prayer as it has been practised in the Church, we might rather consider whether this is not the most neglected area of Christian ethics in our world today. The greatest impact of such ethics, the strongest influence of the Christian spirit on the points of tension with which we are all confronted, will not come from pronouncements of the Church, no matter how ecumenical and unanimous; nor from political action, no matter how considered or how heroic; but from the presence of men and women in whom is revealed the presence and power of their God.

Response to the grace of Christ; communion with the love of God: these are experienced by us within the fellowship of the Holy Spirit. Theologically we have seen that Christian ethics are realized within the context of the Church. But what does this mean in our daily life?

It means, in the first place, very simply, that in our daily decisions and our wider responsibilities we are not alone. There is a solidarity of the human race in both the achievement of good and the incidence of evil. But the fellowship of the Spirit means more than this. In the widest sense we experience the community of the Church as a sustaining company of the living and the dead, without whom we cannot be made perfect. We also know it quite concretely in the family, the group, and the congregation, within which we know a sharing and an encouragement that make possible our growth in the Christian life.

The most important shared experience of this fellowship we know as worship. The Christian learns that this is the necessary expansion of his private prayers, and the opportunity for an encounter with God that can have decisive effect on his growth in the Christian life. The worship described by our Lord as "in spirit and in truth" (John 4. 24) is, in fact, worship that has a moral effect upon our lives. There is neither spirit nor truth in perfunctory ceremonies, or elaborate ritual, or intellectual exercises, or mere "togetherness", that have no moral consequences for the participant. True worship, as an encounter with God, provides the inner nourishment and the moral stimulus by which we grow together into what St. Paul calls "the measure of the stature of the fulness of Christ" (Eph. 4. 13).

In true worship we are all aware, to a greater or lesser degree, of being drawn into the world of mystery, of the supernatural, of the eternal. What happens cannot be fully expressed in words and is often best reflected in music and the arts. This is why an entirely luminous worship, in which everything is perfectly clear and understandable in the modern vernacular, and the setting is as obvious as a hygienic kitchen, is not the worship that restores the soul. When we are truly worshipping in the full mystery of the Gospel, then our contact with the Ground of our Being is of far greater relevance for the daily decisions of the moral life than any form of words derived from our theology. This *is* religion – and it cannot be equated with any experience of the secular or natural world.

The average Christian would probably be inclined to express the impact of worship on his moral life in some such words as: "I go to church to recharge my batteries." And it is true that this aspect of our religious practice has an ethical influence that is too lightly dismissed by the smooth satirists of our religious institutions. The "recharging of our batteries" is not, of course, a direct result of moral exhortation from the pulpit, or the communal singing of improving hymns, but the consequence of a total exposure to the Gospel in the fellowship of believers.

But this is only part of the story. We are less apt to reflect on the other beat in the rhythm of public worship – the giving of the self in offering to God. Worship is the commingling of our praise and dedication as we respond to the Gospel of Christ. Adoration is the highest expression of worship, in which the whole of our being is caught up in the movement of human oblation in heaven and on earth. We are wholly directed towards God in communal and self-forgetful praise. It might seem to be the experience most removed from the practical decisions of every day. But when we are in touch with the living centre of all being, when we are truly encountering the God who has created and redeemed the human race, we are in living contact with the source of all goodness, beauty and truth. It is mysteriously true that man tends to become like that which he worships. Therefore when our adoration is directed to the God whose nature and acts we see unclouded in the person and life of Jesus Christ, then it is his love, his purity, his justice, his grace that is reflected by us. "We all," says St. Paul, "with open face beholding as in a glass the glory of the Lord, are changed into the same image from glory to glory, even as by the Spirit of the Lord" (2 Cor. 3. 18).

Nowhere is the ethical power of the encounter with God more clearly revealed than in the sacrament of the Holy Communion. For it is the communion of the Holy Spirit. It is the moment of worship when our actual religious experience touches most closely the ethics of every day. After all, it is the everyday elements of bread and wine, the structure of our daily life in the human family, that are the means of grace in the sacrament. Here at the Holy Table is the divine community, and here is the mystery. Here is the food and drink to sustain us in the Christian way. And here is the supreme adoration, when with the "Holy, Holy, Holy" we acknowledge the One by whose life, death and resurrection we are given the pattern and the power for the moral adventure to which we are called. We can thus understand the words of the Book of Common Prayer that summon the Christian to this sacrament: "Ye that do truly and earnestly repent you of your sins, and are in love and charity with your neighbours, and intend to lead a new life, following the commandments of God, and walking from henceforth in his holy ways; Draw near with faith, and take this holy Sacrament to your comfort."

Chapter Four

ALONE WITH OUR ETHICS

I T is recorded that among the many enterprises sponsored by that restless and unpredictable monarch James the First and Sixth, was a plan to deposit a newly-born infant on the Bass Rock in the Firth of Forth in sole charge of a deaf-and-dumb nurse. The object of the experiment, which fortunately was never carried out, was to discover what language this child would eventually speak. It might seem obvious today that the answer would be — none; but King James was anxious to test a theological opinion according to which the child would infallibly speak Hebrew, the language of the Garden of Eden. What would interest us much more would be the answer to the question: Would such a child, if we concede the possibility of no kind of communication with any other human being, even in sign language, grow up with any sense of right and wrong? And, if so, what would be the content of his morality — what things would seem right and what things wrong? That is the moral question. It has a theological corollary: Would the child have any knowledge of God?

Our answers to these questions will be guesswork, determined by our assumptions about human nature. What is not guesswork is the fact that Christian ethics assumes that morality has a source beyond the conventions and conveniences of human society. Its power to influence human life has derived from the conviction that right and wrong are not mere labels attached to behaviour that is approved or disapproved by the family, nation, group or gang, but reflexions of an ultimate judgment that lies beyond the social contract of humanity. The tragic heroes of Shakespeare have much more on their minds than the fear of offending traditional taboos or incurring the disapproval of society. They move in a dimension of eternal values — the "even-handed justice", the mercy that "is an attribute to God himself", and "the dread of something after death". The Christian tradition has combined with the Hebrew and the Greek to instil the practical belief in moral absolutes that are independent of the flux of human opinion. (It is the absence of this dimension, and not the presence of specific incidents or four-letter words, that constitutes the "immorality" of some modern plays and novels.)

It is thus possible to speak in Christian terms of a "desert island morality". If you were marooned for the rest of your life on a distant island with abundant supplies for all your wants, but absolutely no communication with any human being, would there be any kind of moral obligation you could recognize, any good to be sought, any evil to be avoided? Obviously if morality has purely social roots, if our ideas of right and wrong are determined by nothing else than the pressures of human society, there could be no such thing as "desert island ethics". You would live, once you had shaken off the habits of a lifetime's conformity to accepted standards, exactly as you pleased with no constraints of conscience or ethical ambitions of any kind. You might be bored, since you could do neither right nor wrong. You might get to the point reached by the frustrated rake who said he was looking for an "original sin". But, on this theory, you would have reached the Nietzschean plateau "beyond good and evil". If, however, we accept the Christian view that right and wrong are rooted in the nature of our God, and that our ethic is related to his will, then your isolation from your fellow men in no way absolves you from responsibility. There is still a good to be sought and an evil to be avoided. There is still the will of God, even in this peculiar situation, to be found and done.

"Desert island morality" may seem a useless hypothesis but it at least directs our attention to a vital element in the impact of Christian ethics on our world. For all the impulses that affect our behaviour in society spring from an inner disposition of heart and mind, the orientation of the will when we are alone with our ethics. In all the contemporary furore about moral codes and Christian principles not much is being said about the lone confrontation of a man with his conscience, or the inward communion of a man with the God whom he trusts. The one is dismissed as "subjective irrelevance" and the other as "outworn piety". Probably no one statement by a modern philosopher has been so often quoted in order to be violently refuted as A. N. Whitehead's remark that "religion is what a man does with his solitariness". Philosophers, historians, sociologists, theologians, and preachers are united in a chorus of condemnation, citing the fundamentally social character of all religion, and Christianity in particular. Yet, if we pause to consider the matter, we surely stumble on a truth in this statement that cannot be denied by any reasonable man with any genuine religious experience at all. Whatever our involvement in the family, the state, the Church, whatever our public profession of faith in word or action, our real beliefs and our real self emerge when we are alone with our God. Surely this is the import of the repeated emphasis of Christ on the decisive nature of our inner disposition, when there is no one around. Our real prayers are in the secret place and not on the street-corner. Our true charity is revealed in the gift that only God can see. Our fasting is to be completely hidden from other people. It is the pure in heart—in the recesses of their solitude—who see God. Our morality is not tested by our adherence to an outward code, but by the solitary disposition of the will. We are told that, for instance, abstention from murder means little compared to the feelings of hatred we nourish in the lonely chambers of the heart. There are moments of supreme loneliness in every human life—when we must reach a grave decision, or when we face the imminence of death—and it is then that our ethical and religious convictions are most critically revealed.

There is thus a hidden factor in much of our public discussion of ethics today. For the deepest springs of moral conduct are not revealed in controversy and debate: occasionally the curtain is drawn back and our secularized society is surprised, or even shocked, to discover the enduring power of Christian ethics in the recesses of the soul. For the decade of the fifties the late Dag Hammarskjöld was the model diplomat, the international civil servant, the skilful negotiator, the typical product of a sophisticated, non-religious society, trained to be "all things to all men" without intrusion of moral or religious scruples that could be identified with any one sector of the human race. We now learn from his private diaries that this was a man who knew how to be alone with his ethics, and with his God; and drew from such communion the strength and inspiration for every detail of his work. The cries of shocked protest that have arisen in some quarters indicate how assured many have been that personal religion with its lonely listening for the will of God is no longer a force to be reckoned with in the ethical debate.

Personal ethics begins with the question of identity. Before we face any questions about our obligations and responsibilities the prior question looms up: Who am I? There is a sense, of course, in which the answer to this question can only be given in our contact with other people. It is within the company of the home, our friends, our community that we discover ourselves. But there must be an identity in solitude, otherwise we shall be like a series of roles with nobody playing them. For in our intercourse with the outside world there are masks to be worn. We are never quite the same person in our family, in our business, in our clubs, in our recreations, in our church, or in the subway. The masks may be false, or they may be true — but they can never be totally discarded, not even on the psychiatrist's couch. For the presence of others always induces a certain response that never totally coincides with the person we know when utterly alone. We are nearest to expressing our real selves with those to whom we are bound in love or close friendship, farthest from it with those whom we know only superficially. In our modern urban societies which are sucking into their maw an increasingly greater proportion of the population of every industrialized country, the range of superficial contacts is constantly extending, so that more and thicker masks are being worn. Thus we have the paradox that the closer people are thrown together the more isolated they feel, for they cannot spend enough time with the man behind the mask. They may even begin to lose the sense of identity altogether and find themselves living on the split-levels of conflicting roles. When Christ asked the wretched lunatic who lived among the tombs in the country of the Gadarenes "What is thy name?" he got the answer "My name is Legion: for we are many" (Mark 5. 9). This is the answer to which modern society is driving us unless we can find a true identity in the place where we are alone. In its extreme form this loss of identity means, of course, severe mental illness, but all of us have some experience of what it means to say "My name is Legion," or, as we might put it today, "I feel more like a committee-meeting than a man."

Our way of life, with its inevitable exposure to the distractions of our mechanized civilization — the mobility of the automobile age, the intrusion of radio and television into every home, the constant invitations of all the media of communication and entertainment — is breeding an increasing reluctance to practise the art of being alone, even a genuine fear of the silence when we are confronted with ourselves. We develop the habit of seizing on the first available alternative to being alone with our thoughts. Magazines, radio, television, trivial conversation, the telephone — anything will do. In case we might be confronted with ourselves before dropping off to sleep we can arrange for a radio with a special switch. It seems that we want to recover an identity in our anonymous society; and yet we do everything we can to avoid the one encounter where it can be found.

If, then, we are caught up in the round of daily role-playing in this way, we are likely to absorb our moral values from our environment. And according to some schools of ethics this is the only place where they are to be found. It is not surprising, there-fore, that there is considerable confusion in the realm of moral values in our society. Every one of us moves in a series of different circles where very different codes of morals often operate. A man may be genuinely moving within a traditional and fairly rigid code when discussing with his son the question of cheating in examinations or with his daughter the subject of pre-marital chastity; but the same man may be moving in a different ethical climate when swapping yarns with cronies at the club, or dealing with his income-tax returns. Again, he may sincerely accept a Christian morality of love and brotherhood from eleven to twelve on Sunday morning, but on Monday evening express the most violent sentiments of racial prejudice. A woman may respect and honour specifically Christian standards within her family circle but unconsciously absorb and acquiesce in a totally different scale of values in the novels she devours. There is a geographical morality which is symbolized by the strait-laced Englishman who, according to legend, always whoops it up during a weekend in Paris. And there is the historical morality which holds that the standards of our grandparents must be respected, but not necessarily observed.

To some extent every one of us must plead guilty to at least a slight shift in standards and expressed opinion as we move from one circle to another. But our moral confusion comes from the existence of these overlapping circles without any centre of authority. Out of this situation there has developed in our day a purely statistical morality, according to which it seems right to do whatever is being done by the majority in whatever circle we are moving. In the realm of sexual ethics the Bible of statistical morality is the Kinsey Report and its progeny. For, quite apart from the accuracy or inaccuracy of these statistics about the sexual habits of twentieth-century western male and female, the implication here is that what so many are said to be doing cannot be called wrong. Every parent has heard the plea: "But everyone in our crowd is doing this or that" or "Everyone thinks this way." And there is no satisfactory answer to be given so long as statistical morality is being accepted in many fields of adult decision. In many quarters the cry is being heard for the restoration of absolute moral standards to bring order out of the moral chaos. But no one seems absolutely certain where these absolute standards are to come from, still less how they are to be imposed. It is easy to orate about them in public meetings, to demand them from the pulpit, to arouse enthusiasm for them at a political gathering. Most sensitive people are convinced that such standards exist, that without them we are given over to increasing lawlessness and immorality, but no one is able to translate such standards into a complete code for twentieth-century life, or willing to suggest that they should be legislated into action.

We must consider this whole question in more detail later. Here we are concerned with the basic question of the overlapping circles in which we move and the conflict of standards among them. We cannot avoid moving in these different circles, but the important point to note is that our moral health demands that they become concentric. That is to say, that there must be one centre of personality out of which we move, and to which we refer the decisions that are to be made in each circle of our activities and interests. In other words, whatever masks we may have to wear, there must be a consistent face behind them. And that face we discover in the lone encounter. The Christian faith is that this encounter is not only with ourselves but with our God.

Suppose we elaborate for a little on the theme of the Prodigal Son. Here is a boy who has an identity as the younger son of a rich and affectionate father. As a child he has no need to wear a mask in the father's presence — as nearly as possible he is himself within the circle of parental love. Then as he grows up he begins to find the whole atmosphere of home stuffy and unsatisfying. He has to wear a mask to hide his increasing resentment. There is that insufferably correct elder brother who always does and says

57

the right thing. His values may be solid and good but to the younger man they seem cramping and confining. So he gets his patrimony and goes off on his own. How many new masks does he have to wear as he makes his way through that lump of money? Every succeeding circle of friends introduces him to new standards and new values. He adopts them all, until he finds himself in Skid Row with no one at hand to prevent the final slide. Then, when he has reached the lowest possible point in the scale of jobs for a Jew — feeding pigs — he finds himself alone in the fields tempted to satisfy his hunger with pig-food. Then, says the Greek text quite literally, "he came to himself". Himself: no mask at all; no distraction to make him forget; no drug or liquor to escape through. Himself: this is the one point from which he can begin to make sense of the different circles through which he has moved. It is here that the moral values will be found, or they will not be found at all — for imposed values have only a limited and temporary use. When he thus "came to himself" he was immediately confronted with the image of his father's house — at first in the quite crude form of physical satisfactions. "How many hired servants of my father's have bread enough and to spare, and I perish with hunger!" (Luke 15. 17). The important point is that simultaneous with his coming to himself was the return to the father, in thought and then in action. "I will arise and go to my father" (Luke 15. 18). The end of the story you know. What concerns us here is the recovery of identity through the father's image, and the recovery of a moral centre through a willing acceptance of the father's will, based on a realization through repentance and trust of the father's love.

The Old Testament story of Jacob wrestling with the unknown stranger at the ford at Jabbok gives us another vivid illustration of the recovery of identity and the overcoming of the sense of alienation that lies at the heart of our moral problems. In this mysterious encounter in the darkness, Jacob, the frightened, baffled, despairing victim of his own murky past, meets the Other who is God — and is given the new name, the new destiny, the new centre from which to act: Israel. In one way or another the Bible reveals to us the basic truth that there is a true self to be discovered, and that it is discovered in the secret place where the masks are off and we are in the presence of our God.

Christian ethics begins here not only because we believe that only God can reveal our true identity, but because the Christian Gospel provides the answer to the fear that makes us shun the divine encounter. At any time the Prodigal Son could have found his way back to the father's home. But he would be sometimes afraid, and sometimes ashamed, for "conscience doth make cowards of us all" and there is a shame that avoids the presence of the holy. The climax of the story is the overwhelming welcome of the father, the running to meet the Prodigal, the embrace, the celebration and the revelry. He claims nothing; and he receives everything. The power of the Christian Gospel resides in something much more than a summons to confront our God: it lies in the assurance of an acceptance that removes our guilt and gives us the new name which is nothing less than Son of God.

The Christian, then, alone with his ethics, is not a timid soul who retreats from the conflicts of the world in order to consult his book of rules. Neither is he a moral hero who devises his own rules as the spoiled child of an indulgent heavenly Father. He is the learner who is discovering what it means to be a Son of God. He knows himself to be the recipient of the grace of our Lord Jesus Christ, to be utterly dependent on the love of God, and that, even in his isolation, he is part of the communion of the Holy Spirit. If the truth begins to dawn on him that the question: "What shall I do?" is indeed answered by the much-debated Augustinian precept "Love God and do what you will", he will both rejoice in the freedom that this revelation gives and be humble enough to realize that he is in the infant-grade in this business of loving God. The instrument through which moral decisions are made in the solitude of the soul is known as the conscience. It is interesting to observe that this word that is so familiar to us in the area of moral decision literally means "self-knowledge". It is through the self-knowledge that comes when we are alone with our God that the sensitivity is given by which we respond to the moral challenge.

Respect for the individual conscience is one of the fruits of the Judaeo-Christian tradition in which we have been raised. We must face the fact that such respect flows directly from the biblical revelation of a self-knowledge that is at the same time God-knowledge. While respect for conscience is often today displayed by those who profess no religious belief, it has yet to be shown that it can survive without the backing of such a faith.

Again, without such backing, conscience can be elevated into a divinity — and since each one of us has a conscience of our own, such a state of affairs is the modern version of polytheism. If conscience is the ultimate criterion in the moral life, if there is no higher judge, we are left with a pantheon of confusion. For we shall have to say that to act according to conscience is always right; which is to say that the court was right that condemned Socrates, that Torquemada was right in his persecution of heretics, that Calvin was right when he allowed Servetus to be burned. The Christian, alone with his ethics, is not alone. With knowledge of himself comes the knowledge of his God under whom his conscience stands. Therefore the Christian knows that his conscience is not infallible. It is his guide to the understanding of God's will. And it is in need of a continuous education.

All this needs to be said in view of the current insistence on the freedom of the Christian conscience, the second half of "Love God and do what you will". It is certainly not a new morality that is being proclaimed when we are reminded that the Christian does not live by a book of rules but by the Spirit of Christ whose sovereign freedom will lead him to new, and sometimes surprising answers of creative love. But this *can* become a new morality when it is divorced from an intense understanding of what "loving God" may mean. As St. Paul discovered, it is highly dangerous to inculcate in any group of people the notion that moral codes can be dispensed with before the conscience has been educated in the love of God. And it could be highly dangerous to lay stress upon the freedom of Christian love at the same time as we loosen the hold we have on the reality and presence of the living God. "Perfect love," we know, "casteth out fear" (1 John 4. 18) but since none of us is yet very near to attaining perfect love a certain fear of consequences is still in order. As we shall see later, in the education of the Christian conscience, the idea of law has still an important part to play.

In the terminology of modern ethical discussion a recurrent word is "responsibility". "Responsible behaviour" has become the *summum bonum* in every field. Employers ask if a candidate for a position is a responsible person. Girls are advised to seek responsible husbands. Students are asked to take a responsible attitude to their studies. In sex mores "acting responsibly" has replaced many of the old taboos. The most damning thing that can be said about a candidate for political office is that he is irresponsible. Now this quality which is so much in demand clearly refers to an inner attitude to life which is at the opposite pole from the indifferent, the selfish, or the "couldn't care less". It suggests the type of person who does not just go through the motions in conformity to what is expected but is inwardly devoted and aware that what he is doing has consequences with which he must reckon. The responsible man, alone with his ethics, is the same person with the same ethics as the one we know on the job. This suggests another word that is commonly used in the current ethical vocabulary—"integrity". When real meaning is attached to this word, which is not always the case, it denotes a radical continuity between the inner and the outer man. He is *one*. That is to say, allowing for the inevitable masks that are worn, there is a consistency between what he is in the secret place and what he is and does in the public arena. Christian ethics finds this quality both taught and exemplified by Christ. Of him alone it could be said that there is perfect identity between his inward attitude and outward acts. And he never ceased to demonstrate how often and how easily we fail to achieve this kind of consistency. This kind of integrity he called having the "single eye" (Matt. 6. 22). Perhaps in a modern translation we shall better hear what he is saying: "The lamp of the body is the eye. If your eyes are sound, you will have light for your whole body; if the eyes are bad, your whole body will be in darkness" (Matt. 6. 22, 23, *N.E.B.*). We learn what this means when we read the ensuing illustration: "No servant can be slave to two masters; for either he will hate the first and love the second, or he will be devoted to the first and think nothing of the second. You cannot serve God and Money" (Matt. 6. 24, *N.E.B.*). The inner eyes are to be so focused that everything is controlled by their light. If they are bi-focal we lose our integrity. There is a centre of the soul where we are alone with our God, and it is from this that light should come to flood every aspect of our lives.

It is clear from this that integrity, as Jesus knew it, depends on a single-minded desire to know and to do the will of God. And there is not the slightest doubt from the records of the Gospels that this is the source and secret of his own integrity. His outward acts flowed in perfect conformity from his inner harmony with the Father in heaven. We are not accustomed to hearing the word "responsible" applied to Christ, but his life and teaching reveal exactly what that word really means. For it is impossible to be responsible without there being someone or something to whom we are responding. The word literally means "answerable", and has no content when the question: Answerable to whom? is left dangling. We know what the answer is in the various areas to which this word can apply. An employer expects a responsible employee to be answerable to him. We expect a responsible statesman to be answerable to his fellow countrymen. But behind all this looms a deeper question that is often implied though seldom elucidated. By "responsible" we denote an attitude to life. A responsible person is one who is responsible, not just for this or that activity, but for his whole life. Then, responsible to whom, or to what? There can be only one answer. The word has a religious origin. We are answerable for our whole life to the God who made us. Christian ethics begins when the voice of God reaches us in our hiding-place — "Where art thou?" (Gen. 3. 9) — and we know that we must respond.

In the second half of the twentieth century any such exposition as this of the inward life of the Christian and the personal response he makes to the presence of his God is bound to raise questions in the field of psychology and psychiatry. For this century has brought a whole battery of new scientific methods of investigating the territory that used to be considered the preserve of philosophy and religion. The words that Christian ethics uses — "conscience", "guilt", "forgiveness", "responsibility", "integrity", and many others — are the raw material of psychological study, and there is a strong parallel between the traditional Christian "cure of souls" and the practice of the psychiatrist. The result is a confusion in many minds. Is religion merely an outdated and picturesque way of saying what now can be expressed with scientific accuracy? Is God an illusion that may, or may not be useful in effecting an integration of the personality? In simple terms, do I take my personality problems to the psychiatrist or to the minister?

A full discussion of the relationship between psychiatry and religion would require another book and a more competent author. But there are one or two observations that ought to be made at this point in our study.

(1) One is that there is not the least reason to fear or mistrust any unbiassed study of the workings of the human psyche. Religion

has no monopoly in the understanding of such things as conscience, feelings of guilt, or the unconscious mind. On the contrary, our understanding of certain aspects of Christian faith and morals has been enriched by the work of modern psychologists. It would be difficult, for instance, for anyone to undertake a serious study of Christian conversion without paying attention to what psychology has to say about the phenomenon of conversion from its point of view.

(2) In the same way, there is no need to assume that a person who has recourse to a psychiatrist has thereby disavowed the validity of his religious experience. That the couch has replaced the confessional, and the psychiatrist the pastor, is a frequent statement in our day, implying that there is a clear choice between religion and psychiatry as therapy for the soul. It is, however, no more true to say that my friend who goes to a psychiatrist with a mental disturbance has renounced his faith than that I have done so when I take a torn cartilage to the surgeon. If Christians believe, as they do, that God works through the therapy of physicians and surgeons towards our restoration to health, there is no reason why they should not believe the same about psychiatry. There is, however, this difference between the two therapeutic practices. Psychiatry deals very definitely with certain areas of belief that are sensitive ones for the Christian. And also we must remember that psychiatry is still far from representing an assured and generally agreed body of teaching.

(3) We have therefore to keep in mind some factors which are often ignored. The most important of these is that psychiatry *per se* can make no affirmation, positive or negative, about the being of God. It is sometimes assumed that because, for instance, Freud was an avowed atheist, psychology has discovered some scientific proof of the non-existence of God. This is sheer nonsense. Neither psychology nor any other science (including theology) can scientifically prove or disprove God. Of course, psychology has produced a new set of reasons which seek to explain why we believe in God — he is a father-figure, a product of wishful thinking, etc. But these explanations can nearly always be used in reverse: we can demonstrate that similar reasons explain why this particular psychologist does *not* believe in God. We have to distinguish between the psychic mechanism of our religious beliefs, which is open to the investigation of science, and the reality in which we

believe, which is not. The God of the Bible revelation who says, "I have made the earth, and created man upon it: I, even my hands, have stretched out the heavens" (Isa. 45. 12) is not subject to the scrutiny of his creatures, or to be laid out on a couch for our investigation. The psychiatrist may explain to me a great deal about what is going on in my mind and soul when I pray, but he cannot tell me there is no one there. He has no instrument or competence to do so.

(4) Finally, we must return to the question of our human responsibility. Dr. John Baillie in his book *Our Knowledge of God* opens with a picture of his childhood. He was conscious, he says, of being responsible to his parents. He was under their eye, and subject to their care and command. But, even at an early age, he also knew that his parents were not autonomous beings. (I doubt if even John Baillie used that expression in childhood.) He sensed that somehow his parents acted as though they themselves were responsible to someone else. And, since his parents were Scottish Highland Presbyterians, there was not much doubt in his mind as to who that "someone else" was. Now, before any amateur psychologist begins to discover some kind of transference, or invoke a father-image, we must ask: is there not a sheer necessity for an ultimate authority to whom all are responsible? However we may be prepared to conceive of such an ultimate authority, it is surely clear that when it is lacking, some lesser authority will take its place. We know what happens when a psychiatrist – or a minister – begins to "play God" with another person's life. The only sure way to avoid "playing God" is to have a deep, a humble, a truly responsive faith in God himself. The strength of the Christian, alone with his ethics, is that he is in touch, however fitfully and partially, with the one God, the source of all goodness, truth and love, and with Jesus Christ his only Son our Lord, in the world-wide communion of the Holy Spirit.

Chapter Five

THE ETHICAL NATURE
OF THE CHRISTIAN COMMUNITY

IT has been necessary to examine the personal and intimate nature of our ethical impulse for the simple reason that there cannot be Christian ethics without Christians; and there cannot be Christians without an inward allegiance to Christ. This is the truth that has been safeguarded by the evangelical tradition in the Church. When it is forgotten, Christian ethics is regarded as a body of abstract principles, necessary for maintaining the fabric of society but with no impact on the personal life of the individual. Such an impact has even been resented at times as an intrusion into the private area of personal morality. Lord Melbourne, after hearing an evangelical sermon in the early nineteenth century, remarked with indignation: "Things have come to a pretty pass when religion is allowed to invade the sphere of private life." He has not lacked successors in this point of view, chiefly among those whose passion for the application of Christian principles stops short of their own personal lives. As Christ himself so often indicated, it is lamentably possible for us to be scrupulous in maintaining the outward appearances of morality and in upholding the strictest principles, while allowing no light to penetrate the inward corruption. The polished sepulchres that adorned the hillsides of Jerusalem were, he pointed out, inwardly "full of dead men's bones, and of all uncleanness" (Matt. 23. 27). The neglect of personal ethics, however, is not the prerogative of the hypocrite: it is the constant temptation of all who are passionately engaged in movements of social reform and causes of public morality. This century has listed more than one distressing case of men genuinely and successfully dedicated to the highest tasks of public ethics whose private lives have subsequently been revealed to be astonishingly lax.

In the last hundred years, however, Anglo-Saxon Protestantism cannot be accused of neglecting the personal nature of Christian ethics. On the contrary, the evangelical tradition has generally tended to inculcate an almost purely personal interpretation of morality. The Church and its theologians may have moved far from an individualistic understanding of the Gospel, and the clergy may preach themselves hoarse on the subject of our corporate moral engagement and responsibility, but the average citizen of the Protestant western world is still inclined to think that Christian ethics is a matter for the private conscience. In the United States, in particular, the heritage of individualism from the old frontier days combines with a suspicion of any kind of authoritarian dragooning of the conscience, to maintain a vigorous respect for a personal morality with emphasis on the autonomy of the conscience. This is sometimes carried so far as to foster the notion that a man's ethics, like his religion, is entirely his own business. Thus, in the name of tolerance, it is considered both irrelevant and smacking of bigotry to inquire into the moral and religious convictions of a candidate for public office. The logical inference of this is, of course, that both religion and morals are personal idiosyncrasies that will affect a man's course of action as little as his views on growing nasturtiums or his passion for philately.

Though there may be few who would carry individualism in ethics to its logical conclusion, there are many who honestly believe that the solution to all ethical problems from juvenile delinquency to global war is to be found solely in the conversion and Christian education of the individual. They see Christian ethics simply in terms of a personal relationship to Christ whereby the individual accepts the guidance of the moral law and the grace that is offered to produce the Christian virtues in our lives. Every ethical problem then can be reduced to the question of multiplying the number of individual believers. The logic of this has a strong appeal to most of us, and finds frequent expression in remarks like: "If we get these kids converted there will be no more drug-addiction and hooliganism"; "If only the world leaders would all live by the principles of the Sermon on the Mount there would be no more wars"; "We've got to deal with the root of the problem; you can't legislate morality". According to this view Christian ethics will penetrate and influence society solely by the example and devotion of individual Christians. The truth behind this point of view lies in the ultimate importance of the "ethic of the alone" that we have already explored, but it has only to be stated in this exaggerated form for us to suspect that such naïve idealism cannot represent the whole contribution of Christian ethics to the world in which we live.

We must ask, for instance, whether in fact it has been historically true that the multiplication of individual Christian conversions has led automatically to the elimination of social evils. A certain kind of Protestant evangelical revival has been notorious for producing a type of Christian with a most unbiblical scale of moral values. Intense individual piety sometimes has resulted in a morbid concern with such matters as drinking, smoking and gambling, and an almost total unconcern with elementary questions of social justice such as fair wages, decent housing and civil rights. The blunt fact is that where evangelical zeal has really influenced society in a major area of human betterment corporate action has always been taken, usually involving legislation. In the days of child-labour in England there must have been many Christian employers who were concerned with the welfare of individual children drawn to their attention and would be willing to offer help in cases of extreme distress. But no multiplication of individual Christian consciences could deal with a vicious situation where infants could be worked, often to death, in factories and mines. The evangelical conscience produced eventually a corporate action through which acts of Parliament were passed prohibiting the evil practice. Similarly in the days of slavery in the United States it was undoubtedly true that individual Christian masters treated their slaves with consideration and even with affection; and the argument was steadily used that there would be no trouble if only each individual behaved in a Christian way. But the individual conscience was incapable of dealing with a fundamentally immoral situation, and only corporate action and legislation freed the slaves. This does not mean that the Christian conscience can *only* be expressed in society by means of public demonstration and social action – in fact, without the backing of a deep personal allegiance and obedience to Christ, such action can become a substitute for religious conviction in a time of spiritual confusion – but it does reveal that the problems of society cannot be solved entirely in terms of individual conversion. There are social evils that require social action, and the Christian ethic has to be expressed corporately as well as individually. It is a notorious fact that the very considerable revival of personal religion evidenced in the United States since World War II, through increased membership in the churches and unprecedented response to mass evangelism calling for personal decision, has coincided with an alarming increase in the crime-rate and social evils of all kinds. It is as if we were being warned that a purely private interpretation of the Christian ethic is incapable of exerting a major influence on the moral health of a nation.

We must indeed begin to suspect that the whole idea of a purely individual ethic, whereby each one responds in isolation to the demand and the succour of the Triune God, is neither practical nor biblical. We cannot experience the grace of our Lord Jesus Christ, we cannot live in dependence on the love of God, without the fellowship of the Holy Spirit, the community into which we are called and without which we are lost. There must be some cohesion of faith in which we discover the ethical strength to influence society. Otherwise personal Christian ethics will lead to moral anarchy. The editor of the Book of Judges, that sanguinary record of social upheaval and tribal infighting, ends his work with the plaintive and semi-apologetic remark: "In those days there was no king in Israel: every man did that which was right in his own eyes" (Judges 21. 25). Whatever our interpretation of the institution of kingship (and there is more than one represented in the Bible records) it is obvious that this "people of God" had discovered the hard way that the individual conscience is not sufficient to hold together the fabric of society. There is a profound need for an instrument of social cohesion. The individual conscience needs the support and enlightenment of a responsible community.

All this is very elementary sociology, and there is a whole range of questions concerning the dynamics of society, the structures of power, group-psychology and the solidarity of the human race into which we could enter if we had the time and competence. What concerns us here is the fundamental basis of Christian ethics, and our source-book is the Bible. Unfortunately the renewed understanding of the Bible as a community document, and of the Church as something much more than the aggregation of individual Christians, which has stimulated the theological world in recent years has not yet penetrated very deeply into the thinking of the average Christian. It is still often supposed that the Bible consists largely of stories of individual encounters with God and of precepts addressed to the private conscience, and that the Church is little more than a convenient grouping of those who share this kind of experience and roughly agree on the precepts. Therefore discussion about social problems is apt to proceed from the assumption that we can simply project the moral demands of the individual on to the wider screen. I accept the obligation to "do justly, and to love mercy, and to walk humbly with thy God" (Mic. 6. 8) and attempt to translate as many of the sterner precepts of Christ into action as I find possible. Then I indulge the hope that somehow the gangster, the hate-monger, the dope-addict can be persuaded to do the same; and that somehow, somewhere, the problems of the world can be settled when Mr. Breshnev, Mr. Johnson and Mr. Mao Tse-tung sit down at a table to thrash out their differences on the basis of the Sermon on the Mount. Such contemplation inevitably breeds a certain cynicism in the best of us, and we are thrown back on the hope that if decent, God-fearing individuals will do their best, laws can be devised and utilized to take care of the rascals.

What is missing in our thinking is the concept of a community where ethical ideals can be realized, and where the individual finds his moral identity and strength. We are, of course, aware that the Bible has much to say about our neighbours and that Christian ethics involves an all-embracing concern for the whole of humanity, but we find it exceedingly difficult to relate our individual moral convictions to the three billion inhabitants of the globe. We realize that the next important question that occurs in the Bible after God's call to Adam, "Where art thou?" (Gen. 3. 9) is the guilty one from the mouth of Cain, "Am I my brother's keeper?"(Gen. 4. 9); but, if we assume this responsibility, where does it end? Is my brother in Harlem, in Hong Kong, in Hanoi? If so, what can I do about looking after him? Individual-istic ethics is powerless before the demands that go beyond the brother at home, or next door, and our Christian love in the wider scale tends to evaporate into a mild feeling of universal benevolence. We succumb to the tendency to retreat to the area of our immediate personal concerns of home and work and neigh-bourhood and to leave the thorny questions of world peace, over-population, malnutrition, social justice, and the like to the operation of political and economic forces, buttressed by our languid prayers and occasional financial contributions. We discover the truth that was so powerfully elaborated in Reinhold Niebuhr's *Moral Man and Immoral Society* — namely, that the Christian ethic of love can be experienced in the home or among a small group of like-minded friends; that it becomes weaker as soon as one group is dealing with another; that it seems largely irrelevant in the context of national policies; and that it is almost wholly inoperative in the relationships between nations. We conclude that Christian ethics is really a matter of our own personal behaviour from day to day and despair of any application in the wider groupings of society.

There is a middle factor in our ethical situation that needs to be recognized and experienced if we are to exert a truly Christian influence on modern life. This is the community of the Spirit that in the New Testament is expressed by the Greek word *Koinonia*. In recent years two Greek words have increasingly occurred in modern writing and speaking about the faith — *Koinonia* and *Agape*. Since their use is often felt to be a sign that the speaker is indicating his familiarity with the vocabulary of a theological "in-group" these words can be an irritant rather than a help. The man in the pew feels he ought to know what they mean but doesn't, while the man in the streets finds them sheer gobbledygook. The excuse for their appearance in English is simply that the traditional translations have too many, and too misleading connotations. The word "love", with its range of meaning from eroticism through romance and charity and senti- ment to the purest altruism, is clearly inadequate to convey what the New Testament means by *Agape*, which is the supreme quality of the Christian ethic — the outgoing, self-giving for others that characterizes both the Christian God and the Christian man. For the original New Testament "*Koinonia*" we are limited to either "communion" with its vaguely mystical associations intelligible only to the initiated, or "fellowship" which is now irretrievably lost in an atmosphere of soft drinks and buns. (The last infirmity of a noble word, and the final linguistic horror, is the verbal form "fellowshipping together".) So, until an English word appears or is rescued from bad company, it may be necessary to employ the Greek "*Koinonia*". Provided we know what we are doing it is not unforgivable to use a unique and strange word for a unique and strange reality.

Koinonia is what happened at Pentecost. There is no better example by which to understand Christian ethics. To our modern way of thinking what should have happened at that time is something like this. A number of individual men and women who had become disciples of Christ decided to hold a meeting. They discussed their religious experience and the moral implications of their new commitment, and decided to found a society for the propagation of the Gospel and the inculcation of Christian morals. They reached agreement on certain principles, elected officers, and began an ambitious campaign for the conversion of individuals throughout the Roman Empire. What really happened was entirely different. These men and women were already united in the company of disciples. They met instinctively for prayer together. While they were, as the Book of the Acts says, "all with one accord in one place" (Acts 2. 1) something happened that they could neither plan nor control. The Holy Spirit, the living presence of God, indicated his presence in a unique and shattering way — and they knew themselves to be bound together in a unity they had never known before. The grace of the Lord Jesus Christ was no private gift any longer; it was upon them all. The love of God enfolded them all. And they could only later describe what happened as the *Koinonia* of the Holy Spirit. They were men and women open to one another, dependent on one another, supported by one another. Their first act was to move out into the world. They spoke to the crowd outside through the mouth of Peter, and when there was a remarkable response to the message it is not described in terms of men and women being converted to Christ and then joining the *Koinonia*. We read simply that "there were added unto them about three thousand souls" (Acts 2. 41). Being a Christian, then, at the very beginning of the mission, meant much more than an individual decision to accept the way of Christ. It meant being absorbed into the *Koinonia*. The Christian way of life developed, not by individual interpretations of the teaching of Jesus, or by attempts to relate Christian precepts to the problems of the Graeco-Roman world, but by experience of the *Koinonia*.

This is the creative middle factor in Christian ethics. If we seek the answer to the question: What shall I do? we are not simply thrown back on our conscience, nor can we turn to the Bible for an exact instruction in every case. We find the answer in the context of the *Koinonia*. If we want to know the reality of the *Agape*-ethic as a way of life in our own day and circumstances, it is in the *Koinonia* that we discover it. If we are looking for a cohesive Christian impact on the intractable problems of society it is the *Koinonia* that becomes for us the instrument of such ethical penetration.

It is clear that this *Koinonia*, though a new reality as the continuing presence of Christ on earth through what came to be called his "new body", is related to the entire content of the Bible. For this unique collection of writings — historical, poetical, legal, prophetic, didactic, devotional — is not a haphazard omnibus collection of the writings of religious geniuses. It is the creation of a community — in the Old Testament the community of Israel, in the New Testament the Christian Church. The individual books, no matter how distinctive their style and personal their contents, are written by men who knew themselves to be members of a distinctive community, and the editing, preserving, and compilation of the respective collections known as the canon of the Old and of the New Testament, were the work of the community. In both cases this literary deposit is something very different from a series of ethical instructions to guide Jew and Christian in their search for the good life. It speaks first and foremost, not of the things that man must do, but of the things that God has done. The Old Testament continually declares that the living God is in action, that he has delivered his people, that he has a purpose for them among the nations of the earth. The New Testament even more emphatically speaks of the new action of God, of the deliverance in Christ, and the purpose he has for the Church in the world. In both cases the ethics flows from an understanding of God's action, and is disclosed within the life of the community.

The middle factor in Biblical ethics can then be described by a whole series of terms that convey this sense of ethical solidarity — "the kingdom of God", "the family of God", "the holy nation", "the people of God", "the Church", "the *Koinonia*". These terms are not identical in meaning, but they all convey the idea of the community within which our ethical response is sustained and developed. In talking about "Christian ethics" today we have to keep in mind that the communion of the Holy Spirit, the *Koinonia*, is still a reality, that our understanding of the Bible is dependent on it, that our experience of *Agape* is born within it, and that the Christian impact on today's world is realized through its presence.

In the Atomic Age today, with its intense conflicts generated by our very gregariousness, with the sense of isolation and alienation growing in many hearts and minds, with the increasing desire of individuals "not to be involved", where are we to look for the evidence of the presence of the Christian *Koinonia*? The simple answer that the *Koinonia* is the organized Church as we know it is not justified either by our experience or the evidence of the Bible. In the early days the Church was a compact minority whose members were very conscious of their unique "membership one of another", and whose impact on pagan society was often sharp to the point of conflict. *Agape* was such a living reality that the tribute of the pagan world was in those days, without any trace of sarcasm: "See how the Christians love one another." But even in those days, when Church membership was strenuous and costly, there is testimony that not every local Church was by any means pure *Koinonia*. From the beginning the organized Church had within it elements destructive of the *Koinonia*, and therefore of the ethical impact of the community, as we see clearly from the correspondence of St. Paul with his Corinthian Church. When the Church settled into a majority position of prestige in the Roman Empire, and still more when it came to dominate the whole of mediaeval Europe, it was still more obvious that *Koinonia* could not be equated with the dominant religious organization of the day. In modern western Europe or America we should be reluctant to suggest that either the multifarious denominations or the local congregations could be simply identified as the *Koinonia* of the New Testament.

It is possible to answer this question by reference to a spiritual reality such as is suggested to our minds by a phrase like "the communion of saints", or "the Church Invisible". It is true that our ethical life as Christians is bound up with our participation in a mystical fellowship from which we draw inspiration and support. "Wherefore," said the author of the Epistle to the Hebrews, "seeing we also are compassed about with so great a cloud of witnesses, let us lay aside every weight, and the sin which doth so easily beset us, and let us run with patience the race that is set before us . . ." (Heb. 12. 1). Every sensitive Christian is aware of

73

his membership in a divine community in heaven and on earth whose worship he shares and whose resources he shares. In our moral life today we can experience what T. S. Eliot has called "the backing of the dead", as well as the encouragement of the world-wide community of prayer and worship. Yet it is clear from the New Testament that the *Koinonia* is experienced also as a concrete reality in the visible Church. What is called the "body" of Christ on earth cannot be etherealized. It is "body" because it is visible, flesh-and-blood, real and near. The middle factor in our ethical situation is a community that can be seen and heard.

We find in the Bible that the true family of God is never simply identified with an institution. In the Old Testament the nation of Israel which is called to be the holy nation, the "people of God", continually refuses its destiny and fails to be the redeeming society in the world, yet it is made plain that within the nation there is always a minority who fulfil this function. The prophets speak frequently of the "remnant" of Israel, the group in which the religious and ethical tradition is alive, and who are responsive to the call of the living God in each new situation. The history of the Church from the Book of the Acts onwards reveals the existence of a *Koinonia* that is not conterminous with the organized Church. The visible Church functions as an ethical guide and a custodian of the moral traditions of the faith. It also provides in its ministry the resources a Christian needs for his moral life and engagement in the world. Such guidance and support is offered by the Church in varying degrees of faithfulness or purity throughout the centuries. But there always exists within it the *Koinonia*, the organic and more intimate fellowship within which Christian ethics comes alive.

This middle factor is experienced in various ways within the wider family of the Church. Most commonly it is realized in the Christian family, and in the communion of friends who share the faith. It is also, however, a real part of the life of any true Christian congregation. It may be that most modern city congregations are too big and amorphous for this *Koinonia* to be vividly felt, yet we must guard against the idea that it is to be sought solely in the company of like-minded people. The specific nature of the Communion of the Holy Spirit is that it does not depend on like-mindedness, still less on common background and social parity. In the *Koinonia* we are given our neighbours; we do not choose them. And they are the neighbours that we learn to love as ourselves. A congregation, or some other grouping of Christians, is the environment in which Christian ethics comes to life and thereby makes its impact on a community, and on the world.

This conception of *Koinonia*, of a Church, of a people of God raises serious questions that demand some answer. It would seem to lend itself to objectionable notions of superiority, group-righteousness, and of a double ethics standard. It is shocking to most of us to read Old Testament passages which seem to imply that goodness and mercy are the perquisites of Israel, and that heathen nations need not be treated in the same way as the people of God. It is in dealing with the outside world that the Psalmists lose our sympathy. They seem to come off the high moral plane and indulge in fulminations of rage and revenge. In the New Testament it has been remarked that we seem to descend in the Epistles to a lower and more restricted level of *Agape* at times, compared with the universal note in the teaching of Jesus. Our Lord speaks of God's universal care for the just and the unjust. When asked to define a neighbour he told a story in which the neighbour of a Jew turned out to be a member of the despised race of the Samaritans. In his word-picture of final Judgment he made our response to the needy, regardless of their race or faith, the test of true compassion. The writers of the Epistles often seem concerned to draw a distinction between "love of the brotherhood" and our behaviour to those outside. Peter's statement, "Honour all men. Love the brotherhood" (1 Pet. 2. 17) corresponds to a general insistence on a specific form of love within the *Koinonia*.

It has to be admitted that *Koinonia* is liable to distortion and deflection from its true purpose. Just as the election of Israel could be misinterpreted in terms of racial superiority and religious prestige, it has been only too possible for Christian *Koinonia* to develop qualities of ingrowing piety, or self-conscious righteousness. But the prophets and apostles witness consistently to the real purpose of the calling of the people of God. They are to be the community that lives for others, that suffers for others. The purpose of the call of Abraham was that in him "shall all families of the earth be blessed" (Gen. 12. 3). The purpose of the call of the Church was that the disciples of Jesus should be witnesses "unto the uttermost part of the earth" (Acts 1. 8). The emphasis in both instances is on service in the deepest sense of that word –

the service that is demonstrated by the Passion of Christ. It is into such a *Koinonia* we are called, not as God's favourites but as his servants, and the servants of our fellow men. And without the existence of such a *Koinonia* our ethical impact on the world would be of little account.

When the distinction is made that we should "love the brotherhood" while "honouring all men", we are not being given a double standard of ethical conduct, although at times the apostles seem to have come close to this in their admonitions. We are really being reminded where it is that we ought to experience the reality of *Agape* as set before us in the ethics of the Sermon on the Mount. It is within the family, whether a literal family or the family of God, that human beings actually experience the mutual self-giving and utter limits of forgiveness that are exemplified in the teaching and parables of Jesus. It is there that *Agape* is generated in the power of the Spirit to become the dynamic of our moral life. Within the *Koinonia* this spontaneous and creative love that needs no law is a reality in a way that it cannot be in the outside world. We cannot then immediately transfer the conditions of the *Koinonia* to the society in which we live. Yet the Word of Christ reminds us that it is the whole world that is potentially the family of God. The *Koinonia* has an open end and cannot be shut without betrayal of the Spirit who gives it life. Therefore Christ's unforgettable picture of the Neighbour remains to stimulate the conscience and remind us of the ultimate *Agape*. Our neighbour is the one we meet, whoever he is, and our ethical duty to him is love, which is interpreted as the caring for his needs even as God cares for us.

This middle factor of Christian ethics – the *Koinonia* that comes between our personal morality and its application to the problems of the world – is then the chief means by which we realize the *Agape* of which the New Testament speaks and also the ethical support and dynamic in our impact on the world. But we do not simply live within the *Koinonia*. We are citizens with responsibilities to our community, to the nation, and to the modern world. We have decisions to make in areas where the *Agape* of the *Koinonia* is not the rule of life. We have to consider what our duties are under a rule of law. In short, we have to ask what Christian ethics has to say about our responsibilities and duties in what is called secular society. To that we must give our attention next.

Chapter Six

THE IMPACT OF
CHRISTIAN ETHICS IN SOCIETY

THERE is a term that keeps occurring in recent books, articles, and sermons — "post-Christian". We hear of a "post-Christian society" in which we live, of the "post-Christian civilization" of the west, and of "post-Christian ethics". Attaching the prefix "post" has always been a neat way of hastening the demise of any movement we disapprove of, but in this case it is usually the friends of Christianity who employ the term. We are being asked to accept the fact that the basic religious and moral ideas of Christianity are no longer generally accepted in the society we live in. Exponents of the faith describe with a kind of relish the extinction of the last vestiges of what used to be known as Christendom, and insist on the incapacity of organized religion to make any serious dent on the neo-pagan assumptions of our world. This Christian masochism sometimes goes so far as to leave the impression that the only possible slogan for the twentieth-century Church is: "Back to the catacombs."

It is probably true that the average church member under-estimates the extent to which modern society is governed and controlled by sub-Christian, non-Christian, and even anti-Christian assumptions. The more clearly we see the avowedly anti-Christian nature of the Communist state in its recent expansion throughout the world, the greater has been the tendency to assume that the non-Communist world is *ipso facto* Christian. We have therefore been blinded to the encroachments of what may loosely be called "secularism" and "materialism" in their western disguises. The existence of a Wall that seals off East Berlin does not automatically make West Berlin a Christian society — and that symbol speaks for the whole east/west situation. No one examining the nature of our modern society, east or west, would be inclined to say that twentieth-century civilization reflects anywhere on earth the clear imprint of the Kingdom of God.

77

Government proceeds nowhere on the basis of undiluted Christian ethics. Contemporary art only very occasionally reveals a Christian understanding of man. The affluent society, with its "conspicuous consumption" and "planned obsolescence", is scarcely modelled on the New Testament. Mass entertainment caters on the whole to standards of taste and value that have nothing to do with traditional Christian morality. We deceive ourselves if we imagine that the ethics of the Christian community are happily reflected in any modern state, or that we are somehow immune to the penetration of pagan philosophies and ideals.

Yet the expression "post-Christian" is misleading. In the first place, it ignores the very real residue of Christian conviction and ethical influence that still exists in many areas of modern society. It is easy from an ivory tower to make a cold analysis of the non-Christian forces that dominate and control the political, economic, and cultural structures of the modern state. But contact with real people — politicians, leaders in industry and labour, artists, scientists, writers — will reveal that the men and women who are responsible for the trend of society are by no means uninfluenced by Christian traditions or by personal Christian conviction. And the pressures brought to bear on the so-called "centres of power" by the public opinion of a democracy still include in many countries what we know as the Christian conscience. In the second place, the expression "post-Christian" implies that until recently there existed such a thing as a Christian society, a Christian civilization; and that is a supposition that deserves examination.

It may be that an historian of the year 3000 might be able to mark a section of western history from about the fifth to the mid-twentieth century as the period of "Christian Civilization", on the grounds that during this period the Christian Church was a dominant cultural influence, Christian values were implanted in education, Christian themes made the subject of art, and Christian thinkers — Augustine, Aquinas, Calvin — the moulders of society. But no one could maintain that at any period whatever there existed a Christian state, in the sense that the total life of a people was ruled and guided by the *Agape* of the New Testament. A Christian society implies that the *Koinonia* is conterminous with the state — that government, industry, law, art, activities of all kinds, are an expression of the communion of the Holy Spirit that is the context of Christian ethics. Both Roman Catholics and

Protestants have made efforts to claim the achievement of a Christian society, but where the claim has been strongest we are least likely to concede it. For neither mediaeval Europe, nor modern Spain, nor Calvin's Geneva (which John Knox pronounced "the most perfect school of Christ yet seen on earth") nor the Puritans' New England, appear to us to be true reflections of the *Koinonia* of the New Testament. In fact, it would appear that the more determined Christians are to create a Christian society the more certain they are to betray the *Agape* of the Gospel and employ the weapons of force and compulsion.

We have thus reached a critical point in our study of Christian ethics and its impact on society. We have to ask what the true relation is between our Christian convictions (and the *Koinonia* in which they find expression) and the wider society in which we live. Society can be called Christian, the state can be called Christian, government can be called Christian, the world can be called Christian only in the sense that Christ has died for all and is risen to be the true King and Head of all creation. In the eyes of a believer, that is to say, they are Christian in the sense that they belong to Christ — even when he is not acknowledged or obeyed. But in the sense of *Koinonia* they are not, and never have been, Christian. In the New Testament the Christian community is clearly distinguished from the world. "They are not of the world", we read in the prayer of Christ in the Fourth Gospel, "even as I am not of the world" (John 17. 14). Yet they are *in* the world. They do not live an enclosed existence in some spiritual vacuum. "I pray not that thou shouldest take them out of the world, but that thou shouldest keep them from the evil" (John 17. 15). The Christian, then, is not only a member of the Church, in the sense of the Community of the Spirit, the *Koinonia*; he is also a citizen of the world — what the New Testament calls the *Kosmos*, the social life of mankind with its groupings in communities and nations, its government, its laws, and its common obligations. This perfectly obvious fact lies at the root of an immense number of questions that have disturbed the Christian conscience from the earliest days until now. The questions are familiar to us all. Samples are: "What loyalty does a Christian owe to a pagan state?" "To what extent should a Christian participate in the activities of a non-Christian community?" "Ought a Christian to protest against national policies that run counter to his ethical convictions?" "To what extent can society be Christianized?" "Is the world a doomed society from which individuals have to be rescued in the ark of the Church, or is it potentially the Kingdom of God on earth?" "What recognition should the state give to the Church?" "Should the Church be concerned with social and political affairs that are the responsibility of the state?" "Can Christian ethics be the basis for legislation?" "Are there two systems of ethics — one for our membership in the *Koinonia*, and one for our duties as citizens?" "Should the Church confine herself to individual evangelism or can the structures of society be converted?" "What means are legitimate for Christians to use in their impact on society?" "Is the true Church perpetually a radical minority in any society in constant tension with the world, or is she able to be in any sense the conscience of a nation, living in general harmony with a government that is well-disposed?"

The fact that these questions are being still debated shows that there is no general agreement on the nature of the Christian impact on human society. At one extreme lies the view that the world, as represented by organized society, is hopelessly evil, and that the Christian must have as little as possible to do with it, rejecting its culture, its politics, its fashions, its ideals, and — as far as possible — its demands. This theory is represented by those sects which claim to be the sole elect, and whose adherents strive to avoid any method of identification with their fellow citizens such as the use of the vote, participation in military service or national demonstrations of any kind, or indulgence in any popular relaxation or amusement. Normally members of such sects are not forbidden to extract such rewards as they can from the evil world, and they are never wholly agreed as to where the line can be drawn between what is worldly and what is not. There is, in fact, no logical way of denying citizenship in the world, short of withdrawing from society altogether — and even a desert island community of the "elect" would soon develop some of the features of organized society as we know it. It should suffice to say that the New Testament gives no support to the view that Christians have no obligations to the authorities of this world. We have to render to Caesar the things that are Caesar's.

At the other extreme lies the view that the Christian Church is destined to penetrate the world, to convert its institutions, and by the deployment of sufficient faith and skill and appropriate social action, to create on earth the perfect society that can be called the Kingdom of God. From this point of view the world is not a corrupt society from which we are to be rescued, but a system that can be steadily Christianized. Hence its adherents enter vigorously into the life and politics of the world and are apt to identify any idealistic movement as a sign of the coming Kingdom. They are notorious for their underestimation of the sinful factors in all human groupings, the corruption of power in all human government, and the difficulty of deciding what are true Christian goals for a nation. Christians with this naïve understanding of their relation to the world have not only backed movements and legislation as sure signs of the coming Kingdom, but have, in the opinion of many of us, often conspicuously backed the wrong horse, e.g. Prohibition in the twenties, and Pacifism in the thirties. It is again sufficient to say that there is no warrant in the New Testament for the view that the world is a garden whose weeds can be eliminated by appropriate social action, or that human society and its institutions can be converted by the legislation of agreed Christian ethics.

Between these two extremes of total rejection and total acceptance of the world lie a whole series of theological attempts to relate the Christian to society, the *Koinonia* to the *Kosmos*. These have derived from particular interpretations of Scripture, from differing doctrines of the nature of the Church, and from specific historical situations. There have been theories that stress the tension that must exist between the *Koinonia* and the *Kosmos*, in which the emphasis is laid on the apostolic declaration: "We ought to obey God rather than men" (Acts 5. 29); the Church is viewed as a prophetic minority charged with declaring the pure Christian ethic and resisting the contamination of secular society, and government is regarded as a necessary evil to be accepted for the preservation of law and order. Theories of this kind, while not rejecting the *Kosmos* and renouncing all civic responsibilities, have conceived of the *Koinonia* as a kind of holy nation within an unholy nation with which some *modus vivendi* has to be worked out, but against which protest must continually be made. Then there have been theories that are born of the conviction that *Koinonia* can be expanded until it practically coincides with a particular *Kosmos*, that stress the apostolic injunction: "Let every soul be subject unto the higher powers . . . the powers that be are ordained of God" (Rom. 13. 1); that regard the Church as the "soul" of the *Kosmos*, the conscience of the nation, and think of government as promoter of the good and defender of the Church. Such theories usually involve an acceptance of a division of function between Church and state, an allocation of what belongs to God and what to Caesar. Mediaeval Catholicism, Lutheranism, and Calvinism have each in their own way operated on a theory of co-operation between Church and state, of a fruitful relation between *Koinonia* and *Kosmos*, of a twofold obligation of the Christian man. What none of them has solved is the problem of reaching an agreed delimitation of the respective spheres of authority and of obligation. In the mediaeval period there was continual conflict between Pope and Emperor on this very point; Lutheranism has been haunted by the shadow of a political sphere in which Christian ethics is largely irrelevant; and Calvinism has never solved the dilemma of obedience to the magistrate on the one hand, and the right to defy him on the other. In general it could be noted that the first group of theories usually rise out of a minority-situation when the Church is, or feels herself to be, confronted by a pagan state; while the second develops in a majority-situation when the Church has achieved some form of establishment within the nation.

The history of the Christian Church from the time of Constantine to the beginning of the present century has thus revealed a constant struggle to understand the true relation between the *Koinonia* and the *Kosmos*. Ernst Troeltsch, writing in the late nineteenth century, was able to summarize the debate by his famous classification of Church and sect. By "Church" he meant the conception of a *Koinonia* that strove to be all-embracing, practising infant baptism on a national scale, enlisting the entire population, and seeking to enfold the total life of a nation within the Christian community. By "sect" he meant the conception of a *Koinonia* that strives continually to be pure and true to the New Testament pattern, that stresses the difference between its life and the life of the *Kosmos*, that attaches great importance to individual conversion and profession of faith, that is often in open opposition to the policies of the state, and that does not expect society as a whole to conform to Christian ethical standards. Troeltsch does not use the words "Church" and "sect" in their particular meaning in any local situation, but employs the expressions "Church-type" and "sect-type" to designate two different Christian ways of thinking. Any one congregation today may well contain Christians of both types. The categories define two radically different ways of understanding the *Koinonia*. In lands where there is still an established Church it is normal for "Church-type" thinking to predominate, while those who are opposed to it will be found usually within the dissenting bodies, but in lands where there is no establishment the two different views of the Church exist in almost every communion.

It is doubtful if this distinction is going to be helpful much longer. The fact that both views can appeal to the New Testament for support reveals that neither has reached a truly Christian solution. And we are now entering on a period of the Church's history where past guide-lines are of only limited helpfulness. It would seem a reasonable surmise that the "established Church" is on its way out. There are still nations where the century-old tradition of a "national Church", Protestant or Roman Catholic, has still a strong hold on the population, but it is scarcely conceivable that any of the new nations of our time would elect to recognize a Christian Church as the official representative of the nation's religious beliefs. The pattern which has existed in the United States during the major part of its existence is more likely to be the norm for the Church's existence in the modern state. It is strange to find that in the nation with by far the greatest proportion of regular Christian church-goers a fairly rigid doctrine of the separation of Church and state has emerged, which was characteristic of what Troeltsch called the "sect-type", while in Communist-dominated nations of eastern Europe there are still remnants of such state-support as were associated with his "Church-type".

It would be foolish, however, to suppose that the American doctrine of "separation of Church and state" has reached a satisfactory solution of our problem. For, apart from the fact that this doctrine was a later development of the Constitution's simple safeguard against a privileged and established Church, just what exactly does it mean? It has now been ruled that it implies that no kind of religious worship or instruction shall be offered in state-supported schools, but so far it has not been declared that it is unconstitutional to support army chaplains from public funds, to invoke God's name in court or in Congress, or to have

"In God we Trust" inscribed on the coinage. It is probably true that in no other country do the Christian churches wield such influence on the political and social actions of the state. To only a very limited degree can the American point of view be classified as the "sect-type" of *Koinonia*, for the average Christian is certainly not at all conscious of any serious tension between Church and state. "Separation of Church and state" remains a rule-of-thumb for protecting the nation from exploitation by any majority religious group, but it is certainly not generally interpreted to mean that the Christian *Koinonia* is to have no impact upon the structure and goals of the state.

The situation today has not only been changed by the virtual disappearance of the established Church. It is marked by an outlook that transcends the boundaries of the nation-state. In a new way the *Kosmos* is presented to us as a worldwide phenomenon. We are aware of trends of secular thought, concentrations of power, the application of scientific techniques, the striving after material goals, the growth of both governmental and industrial power, that are affecting almost every nation on earth. The *Kosmos* is no longer just the organized society of a particular people. It is, as it must have seemed in the first days of the Church, the world-atmosphere that we breathe — replete with hopes and fears, visions and threats, meaning and absurdity. It is the *Kosmos* with which St. Paul had to do when he said that "we wrestle not against flesh and blood, but against principalities, against powers, against the rulers of the darkness of this world, against spiritual wickedness in high places (Eph. 6. 12). It is this worldwide *Kosmos*, with its element of the demonic, with which we have to deal.

We have concurrently the revival of the worldwide conception of the *Koinonia*. For the Christian is now aware not only of the fellowship of his local church, of his denomination, or of the total Christian community in his nation, but of the Church ecumenical. It is over against the new stirrings of a worldwide *Kosmos*, which contains within it the seeds of chaos, that God is renewing his worldwide *Koinonia*. We are therefore aware that no solution to the question of the relation of Church and state is ultimately valid that is applicable only in America, or only in Britain, or only in Russia, or only in Africa. The strategy of the Church will be different in different segments of the world, but the true relationship of the *Koinonia* to the *Kosmos* has to be discovered on an ecumenical basis. There will be a difference in immediate solutions to our problems according to whether the Church exists in a benevolent *Kosmos*, a hostile *Kosmos*, or a neutral *Kosmos*, but it is important for us to realize that fundamentally we are members of an ecumenical *Koinonia* facing a *Kosmos* that exerts a worldwide pressure on the Christian conscience.

It is not surprising therefore that the New Testament is coming to life again and yielding new insights for our understanding of the Christian role in the modern world. For, although the apostles lived in a vastly different world from ours, they thought ecumenically both of the *Kosmos* and the *Koinonia*. They had no securities provided by the cushion of a "Christian nation". They were aware of the demonic dimension of the Roman *Kosmos*, but also aware of the ethical values of law and order that it embodied. And, above all, they had a sense of the truly cosmic significance of the Lord whom they worshipped. What, then, do we find to guide us in our search for right answers to the questions that are posed by our dual citizenship in the *Koinonia* and the *Kosmos*, in the teaching of Christ and his apostles?

(1) First, we have to face the obvious, but sometimes disconcerting fact that no rules are laid down for a Christian's specific duties in the *Kosmos*. Unlike the Old Testament which legislated in some detail the duties of an Israelite as a citizen — not only the religious, but the moral, social and political obligations — the New Testament has little to say about the duties of a Christian citizen in a pagan state. For instance, Jesus gave no instructions to his followers about their attitude to the Roman authorities except the incidental remark to his interrogators to "render to Caesar the things that are Caesar's" (Mark 12. 17) — which in this case meant paying the Roman tax. Neither he nor his apostles explicitly raised any of what we would call the "social issues" of the day. There is no word about the morality of the institution of slavery, or any explicit condemnation of the methods of a totalitarian government. No question is raised about the legitimacy for a Christian of serving in the Roman armed forces — indeed soldiers seem to receive especially favourable mention both in the Gospels and the Book of the Acts. For this disconcerting silence there are at least two reasons. (a) Christ was founding a *Koinonia*, a new community that was to be worldwide and enduring. Unlike the

old Israel which was based on the idea of a holy nation, a specific people through whom all the families of the earth were to be blessed, this new Israel was to be launched into the world as a supra-national community. As such it would confront the *Kosmos* in all its forms. Specific rules could be given for Israel, the holy nation, in its location in history, but no such rules could be given for the new community which was to make its way across the world and time. (b) It was also characteristic of the *Koinonia*, compared with the old Israel, that it was to confront the *Kosmos* not according to a fixed pattern of laws, but in the freedom of the Spirit, being led to determine its attitude in each new situation. To these reasons for the silence of the New Testament about specific problems of ethics in the society of the day, some would add that the apostolic Church was so dominated by the thought of the early return of Christ, and consequent end of the *Kosmos* they knew, that such matters would appear irrelevant to their task.

(2) The New Testament, however, provides the material for a dynamic interpretation of the *Koinonia*'s impact on the world. You cannot read the words of Christ, the adventures of the early Church as recorded in the Acts of the Apostles, or the correspondence of the apostles without being conscious that this *Agape* which was the life-blood of the *Koinonia* was being directed outward to the *Kosmos*. Jesus' words are explicit: "Ye are the salt of the earth . . . Ye are the light of the world" (Matt. 5. 13, 14). The revolution in the lives of the disciples was to be the instrument of a revolution in the society in which they lived — and they were to live everywhere "in Jerusalem, and in all Judaea, and in Samaria, and . . . the uttermost part of the earth" (Acts 1. 8). Very soon it was being reported of the *Koinonia* that "These that have turned the world (*oikumené*) upside down are come hither also" (Acts 17. 6). The habits and customs of the *Kosmos* were undermined by the new community that was released into human society. Prejudices were dissolved as the inner meaning of the Christian *Agape* was realized. The discovery that the cross of Christ meant that God had not only made peace between himself and men, but between man and man, led first to the overcoming of the hostility between Jew and Gentile. Within the *Koinonia* there was to be no such discrimination. They accepted also that there was within the *Koinonia* to be no discrimination between freeman and slave. It

took eighteen centuries before the conclusion was drawn that slavery itself was a denial of Christian liberty. How much longer has it taken to realize that in the light of the Gospel the colour of a man's skin is of no significance? Christian *Agape* has acted as a kind of time-bomb within the Church, and as it explodes it inevitably affects the Church's impact on the world.

(3) We must next seek an answer to the question of how this impact is to be made on the *Kosmos*. Recent studies of the New Testament have fastened on one key-word in this connection. Church history reveals that a great variety of means have been used for the penetration of the *Kosmos* with the ethic of the Gospel. The worst of these has been sheer force whenever the Church was in possession of political power. In the attempt to convert the *Kosmos* by the methods of the *Kosmos* the ethic of the Gospel was inevitably distorted and destroyed. "My kingdom is not of this world: if my kingdom were of this world, then would my servants fight" (John 18. 36). These words, which have sometimes been taken to mean an absolute prohibition against Christians engaging in warfare, surely refer to the employment of force for the establishment of Christ's Kingdom, for the conquering of the *Kosmos* by the *Koinonia*. The key word of the Gospels relating to the penetrating of the *Kosmos* is not conqueror but *servant*. The Gospels report that astonishing fact that the Messianic title chosen by Christ, both explicitly and implicitly, was "Servant". And without question it is as Servant that the Body of Christ is called to act upon the *Kosmos*. We are only slowly beginning to realize what this means. For physical force is not the only way by which the *Koinonia* can be led to betray its Master. The temptation to create "Christian" political parties, to exploit the emotions of crowds, to seek positions of privilege, to indulge in religious imperialism — all this is ruled out by the Servant concept. We are also under warning that even the best movements of Christian reform are capable of being subverted by the lust for power.

(4) This dynamic of service demands a fresh understanding of our relation to the *Kosmos*. We begin to see that if our task in the *Koinonia* is to serve the *Kosmos* it cannot be the irredeemable enemy doomed to destruction. We hear again the word that "God so loved the *Kosmos*" — not the *Koinonia* — "that he gave his only begotten Son" (John 3. 16). So we learn again what it means to be *in* the *Kosmos* as servants of Christ and our fellow men. The

recent emphasis in theology and ethics on the Christian's identification with the world finds its real root here. To be a servant in the world is to know it as the object of God's love, and to be delivered from the notion that a Christian stays within the ark of the organized Church beckoning feebly to others to join him, and throwing the neediest of them a few coppers. On the other hand if we are to *serve* the *Kosmos* it is equally obvious that we cannot be "of it" — that is, sharing its futility and despair, adopting its standards, and succumbing to its demonism. It is in this sense that we can understand St. James's apparently rather smug remark that we are to keep ourselves "unspotted from the world" (Jas. 1. 27). Here we part company from the modern apostles of non-evangelism who maintain that we should dismount the structures of the *Koinonia*, merge into the moral climate of our times, and adopt the Godless world of our atheist contemporaries as our true spiritual home. The service in which the Christian makes his impact on the world is both the active *Agape* of the individual in the place where God has set him, and the healing function of the *Koinonia* in the local parish, the community, the nation, and the world. It is an identification with the *Kosmos* in its need, and an identification with Christ in his redemptive suffering and triumph.

(5) We may have some understanding of this relationship of service to the *Kosmos* within the *Koinonia*, but what about our response to that other aspect of the *Kosmos*, the demands that are made on us as citizens? Here Christians are asking again what it is that the New Testament is saying to us about the *Kosmos*. We are not satisfied with the glib answer that the question can be settled on the two levels of obedience to God within the *Koinonia* and obedience to Caesar in the *Kosmos* outside. What was Jesus saying with his word about Caesar and God? Surely not that the two have each their autonomous sovereignty, for his whole teaching, like that of the Old Testament before him, refuted any division of creation into God's domain and someone else's. There is not a spiritual world where we are to obey God, and a secular world where we obey the government. Instead the picture he gives is one huge circle enclosing everything that is: this is where we render to God the things that are God's — for everything is his. Then, within this huge circle, there is a little sphere where Caesar has his relative autonomy. This is the area of human

authority. This is the society of which we are a part. This is the state.

It is important to notice that the New Testament, while speaking little of the nation-state as we know it, has much to say about the "powers that be" — i.e. government. It is regarded as divinely ordained. And this divine ordination is seen even when the state is notoriously evil and anti-Christian. The king that St. Peter tells his fellow Christians to honour is probably Nero. Human authority is seen as necessary for restraint on evil-doers and for the maintenance of public order. There is much evidence in the New Testament of the respect of the Early Church for the *Pax Romana*. But it is probable that we are also being told that the state has its positive service to render, and this becomes more likely as the *Koinonia* encourages its members to take active part in the work of government. Within this semi-autonomous area of human authority we can see Christian ethics at work through the practice of justice and the reign of law. Once the function of government is accepted as not only God-given, but in a sense the symbol of the kingly reign of Christ, we can see how justice and law have their place in the Christian impact on the world. We are not to suppose that as members of a *Koinonia* where *Agape* is the supreme rule of life we can have nothing to do with the *Kosmos* where laws are strictly maintained, punishments imposed, and the sanctions of force employed. The Christian impact on the world is not served by undermining respect for the law, by continual attack on what is called "conventional morality", or by indiscriminate resistance to the requirements of the state. *Agape* does not abolish the necessity for justice or the uses of the law. It presupposes them, and in the *Koinonia*, rises above them.

On the other hand, we must note that the demand for ultimate loyalty to God makes it impossible for the Christian or the *Koinonia* to proffer an absolute and final obedience to the state. "Thou shalt worship the Lord thy God, and him only shalt thou serve" (Matt. 4. 10; Luke 4. 8). Hence there is in Christian ethics an embedded right to resistance and refusal to the powers that be. The entire problem of Christians in the *Kosmos* consists in determining the point at which disobedience to its authority becomes imperative. Every Christian Church has expressed in one way or another this ultimate right of resistance. And it is, of course, written into the New Testament along with the commandment for general obedience. The persecutions of the Early Church are reflected in the lurid pictures of the *Kosmos* inscribed in the Book of Revelation. Here the potential demonic qualities of the worldly powers are written large, and in every Christian century there have been martyrs who have chosen to die with Christ rather than to conform to an impossible demand on their Christian conscience. The Christian today has to judge at what point such resistance may be demanded of him. Our answers can only be given within our own situation in the *Kosmos*. No one in the western world can tell a Christian in a Communist country when it is his duty to resist the state. No one in New York can tell a Christian in Alabama exactly what his attitude should be to the authorities with which he has to deal. What Christian ethics implies here for all of us is an awakened sensitivity to the universal nature of the *Kosmos* in its challenge to the Kingdom of Christ, and the courage to resist when we believe it threatens our ultimate loyalty to God.

(6) Finally, we must hear the New Testament summons to the *Koinonia* to be an instrument of both warning and hope. The present era opens up such dazzling prospects for mankind that the temptation of *hybris* — that pride which both Greek and Jew discerned to be at the root of human evil and misfortune — is enormous. Therefore the *Koinonia* is set in the world as the reminder of the sovereignty and judgment of God. At the same time the *Koinonia* rejoices in the divine gifts of the created universe and the unlimited possibilities of redemption. Therefore its word to the world is not simply one of solemn warning against building a new tower of Babel into space, but of hope that, by the grace of God, the *Kosmos* which he so loved may be transformed still farther by him who is both its Redeemer and its Coming King.

Chapter Seven

THE ETHICS OF OUTER SPACE

BEHIND every discussion of ethics today there curls a question-mark that ought not to be ignored. It arises from our dawning apprehension of the kind of universe that modern science is disclosing to us. We have a suspicion that the thinking of past generations about man's behaviour may not be altogether valid in the wide open spaces of today's cosmology, and that the word "God" has no longer quite the same ultimate and authoritative sound that it had for our forefathers. The vast extent of the physical universe, and the relatively insignificant place occupied in it by the planetary system of which our earth is a part, has been common knowledge for several generations, but it is only recently that the picture has begun to take hold of our minds. This is not only because of the usual time-lag between the surface acceptance of a new set of facts and their assimilation into our world-view, but also because in quite recent years the validity and accuracy of the researches of astrophysics have been strikingly demonstrated for us all in the series of spectacular probes into space. It is one thing to realize in the back of one's mind that the astounding statements of the scientists about the extent and nature of the universe are probably true; it is quite another to watch a capsule blasting off towards the moon. Suddenly we are aware that we do indeed cling to a tiny fragment of a solar system, and that these first little leaps into space are the precursors of still more astounding adventures in a new dimension of discovery.

Simultaneously a lot of things are happening to human consciousness — and they have all very much to do with Christian ethics. We wonder, for instance, whether the codes of behaviour that have derived from the Christian Gospel have any kind of validity in outer space, and whether, if there is anything resembling humanity on another planet, it shares any of our ideas about goodness or about God. Such thoughts have suddenly passed from the attic of our idle speculation to the living-room of our serious contemplation. At the same time we are aware that the boost of humanity towards the stars has been made possible by a fantastic development of the atom. So queries arise about the limits of man's power and the ethical controls that are possible and desirable in this titanic break-through in the conquest of nature. We are vaguely suspicious that the traditional roots of our ethics may have been destroyed at the very time when some form of ethical control has become a matter of life and death. On the one hand eloquent writers inform us of the utter insignificance of the human race in the total scheme of things, while on the other we are vigorously exhorted to realize that man has come of age and can now assume a control that used to be the privilege of the gods. All the time we are aware that this torrent of new ideas and experiences is arising from a world that is rapidly unifying and contracting, in spite of ideological division and ebullient nationalism. Ethical questions rise on a global scale — the prevention of nuclear war, the control of over-population, the use of technology to overcome starvation and disease. The sense of enormous expansion combined with stifling contraction produces in us some of the symptoms of anxiety and despair. We know what it is to say with Hamlet: "O God! I could be bounded in a nutshell, and count myself a king of infinite space, were it not that I have bad dreams."

For those peoples whose ethical outlook has been chiefly determined by the Judaeo-Christian tradition, the major effect of the scientific revolution through which we are passing seems to be at this stage a tragically heightened sense of *insignificance*. When it has been really brought home to us that our whole solar system is as a grain of sand on the seashore of the galaxy to which it belongs — a galaxy with a diameter of a hundred thousand light-years which takes three million years to make a revolution — and that billions of other galaxies are swinging in space; and that even the cosmic accident that made life possible on this planet may still be repeated in the universe, even if the odds are a billion to one against it, we may well feel stunned with a sense of our infinite unimportance. A little familiarity with the cosmic, or even the planetary time-scheme makes our books of human history look like the futile analysis of a mere flicker in the chronology of the universe. When we add to this the biological and psychological discoveries that are steadily inculcating the thought concerning our close affinity with the animal world, and the tendency to place all human experience within the framework of scientific law, the significance of our wills and actions shrinks farther still. If there then seems little that is unique or important about the human species, the significance of the individual is under even stronger attack. For the application of scientific discoveries to personal life, while bringing abundant benefits that were denied to our forefathers, has also created an acute sense of insecurity. The average man feels less than ever "the master of his fate and the captain of his soul" when technological skills may be used to manipulate his soul, and thermo-nuclear weapons to determine his fate. It is all very well to say that man has created these powers, and man can decide how to use them, but for practically all of us "man", in this case, is a shadowy anonymous figure with a test-tube in his hand, or his finger on a button.

What this is doing to our ethics is not hard to discern. For every strong ethical system — and the Christian in particular — is based, as we have seen, on a strong sense of significance and responsibility. No one can read the New Testament without hearing the constant note of an intense moral seriousness. The teaching of Jesus and his apostles is addressed to human beings who have a choice to make, and a choice that matters enormously. Not only is there the prophetic insistence on goodness, mercy, and justice as absolute demands on the conscience, but moral decisions are given an all-importance of which the symbols are nothing less than heaven and hell. The replacement of the eternal context by the morally-empty concept of outer space, which has probably happened in more minds than the Church likes to think, is bound to weaken the sense of responsibility and of the ultimate importance of moral decision. When this is joined to the feeling of insignificance induced by our cosmology, biology, and anthropology, and the feeling of helplessness as victims of a technocratic society, the result is an outlook on life in which morality becomes little more than the oil that greases the social circles in which we move. In fact, when any ultimate significance goes out of human activity and behaviour, ethics is reduced to etiquette. And it is our various modern etiquettes that are really the substance of a great many modern novels and plays, which is precisely where they differ from the classical literature of the past. It would, of course, be a gross misjudgment to dismiss modern art as obsession with the trivial, but it is noticeable that in its greatest moments it, with few exceptions, reflects the despair, the confusion, and the sense of the absurd that dominate a society where human action is robbed of true significance. The same response to our loss of any cohesive pattern of meaning in the universe is, of course, to be seen in the extravagances, the irresponsibility, and the delinquency that a puzzled middle-age complains of in the activities – or lack of activity – of the generation behind them. "What's the use?" they say. "Nothing makes sense any more; so let's get the kicks where we can. It's a mad, mad, mad, mad world."

A glance backwards in history will reveal that previous revolutions in our scientific understanding of man's place in the universe have been accompanied by a moral and religious upheaval, and a period of intense restlessness and anxiety. The Copernican revolution by which a prevailing geocentric cosmology was replaced by the familiar picture of our planetary system had repercussions not only in Church and state, but in the way of life of ordinary people. "And new philosophy," writes John Donne, "calls all in doubt." Somehow the adjustment of the mind to a new picture of the universe, while stimulating and liberating for the human spirit, was felt to be threatening to the accepted moral values of a stable and orderly universe of which the earth had been considered the centre. As for the divine sanction behind man's ethics, while nothing so sleek and simple as a relocation of the image of God from "up there" to "out there" took place, there was an outburst of theological activity in which Christian orthodoxy struggled for new expression amid the voices of deism, mysticism, neo-platonism, rationalism, and charismatic movements of all kinds. The scientific discoveries, as they penetrated the thinking of the man in the street, created a certain confusion and restlessness in his religious and ethical outlook. With this, too, went the exhilaration of the explorations to which the scientific revolution prompted the human spirit. There were new worlds to discover and to conquer across the oceans – and who knew what might be found there?

A similar ferment accompanied the scientific explosion that broke in the nineteenth century with the publication of Darwin's *Origin of Species*. Once again the new vistas opened out by the popularization of the new biology and the new anthropology caused an upheaval in the world of morals and religion. It is scarcely necessary now to rehearse the shrieks of despair and anger that arose in some sectors of the Church at what looked like a catastrophic degradation of man. If human beings, it was argued, are now to be inserted into an evolutionary escalator, leading from the primitive slime to some unknown destiny, what becomes of the image of God in man? What about his unique responsibility as a moral being? Do right and wrong, good and evil, and perhaps God himself, evolve too in this all-encompassing process? Is sin now to be regarded simply as the remnant of the beast? And are the prime values to be accepted now strength and adaptability rather than justice, goodness and love? Since many of these questions are now answered to our satisfaction, and others appear to be based on a misapplication and misunderstanding of biological theory, we may smugly feel that our Victorian ancestors were raising a moral and religious tempest in a scientific teapot, but the literary evidence is there to reveal how deeply and permanently a scientific revolution may disturb and change religious and ethical thought.

The current uproar about the extent to which our thinking about God, and the ethical codes and ideals which derive from religious belief, must be revolutionized in the light of the be-wildering advance of modern science needs to be appraised with some calm and historical perspective. It is undoubtedly true that none of us has yet fully grasped the enormity of the changes that are sweeping over whole areas of human experience as modern technology gets to work. No past scientific revolution has ever moved at such a speed, or with such devastating effect, as the present one. The extent of human control over the forces of nature has expanded beyond all previous dreams, and the rate of scientific discovery and technological exploitation has accelerated at a fantastic rate. On the other hand it is equally true that religious and moral ideas are not necessarily caught up and submerged by this fantastic rush into the future. On the contrary the scientists themselves are the first to emphasize that our tremendous strides in the region of "know-how" desperately need to be guided by a clear vision in the region of "know-what" and "know-why". There is no evidence whatever that increasing control over nature is automatically accompanied by the wisdom that knows what use should be made of it. The ends that we should seek do not just evolve out of our skill in discovering the means. Past experience has shown that scientific revolutions have been successful in ridding religion of superfluous baggage of a quasi-scientific nature, and modifying ethical demands that were based on a mistaken or insufficient understanding of the human situation; but none of them has had the slightest effect on belief in a God who is the beginning and end of the whole human story, and from whom we derive both the ethical ideal and the power to respond to it. Therefore, while facing the necessity for radical changes in our expression of the Christian Gospel, and in our interpretation of the Christian ethic, we need not be swept off our feet by the gusts of theological panic and ethical defeatism that blow from some quarters of the Church today.

This question of insignificance, for instance, needs to be examined in the light of a Gospel that is not made irrelevant by any new discovery about the physical universe, or by any new assumption of control over the forces of nature. Whether, in fact, modern cosmology and the anonymous threats posed by such inventions as nuclear power and automation provoke a sense of insignificance or not, depends entirely on the point of view generated by a faith that is not the product of any scientific process at all. Neither militant Communism nor the new forms of nationalism show any signs of being intimidated in their quests by any paralysing sense of insignificance. It is faith, or lack of faith, that determines our response to the realities of the age of space. And of all faiths the Christian, with the ethic that it implies, is most capable of meeting the challenge of the scientific revolution clear-eyed and unafraid.

There is, in the first place, no need for Christian ethics to surrender its belief in the significance of man and the profound meaning of human life under pressure from the cosmology of sheer enormity. If time and distance are considered the highest values in the universe, then naturally man, poised briefly on his little planet amid the immensities of space and time, is of little or no account. But why should these particular measurements be given this status in our thinking? Teilhard de Chardin points out in his essay on "Life and Planets: What is Happening at the moment on Earth?" (*The Future of Man*) that this perspective of sheer size is "not only discouraging for our action, it is also too contradictory, physically, with existence and the exercise of our intelligence (which, after all, is the sole force in the world capable of dominating the world), to be able to be the last word of science".

He goes on to indicate, from a scientific point of view, how much more illuminating for our understanding of the universe is the quality of "complexity". By this he means the appearance of that which is composed of numerous elements, and that which is delicately and intricately organized. From this point of view the least significant items in the universe are those which impress most those who have succumbed to the popular "numbers-game". These are the vast galaxies, composed probably simply of hydrogen. Next to these come the stars, which are already considerably more complicated in structure. Then comes the extraordinary cosmic freak by which a planetary system comes into being and we are in the presence of matter of extreme complexity and elaborate organization. Of all known planets our earth, owing to its situation and cosmic climate, has produced the fantastically complex phenomenon of life. We can then trace again the degrees of complexity and organization through all living forms till we arrive at the living creatures who are composed of some hundred million millions of cells, with hundreds of millions of atoms per cell. From there we finally arrive at man, in whom the whole process of complexity and organization reaches not only its highest level, but attains consciousness, or self-reflection.

On purely rational grounds it would seem that there is more reason to be astonished at the phenomenon of man than at the immensity of the galaxies, more reason to be impressed with the brain that explores the universe than with its vision of the infinite emptiness of space. From the point of view of Christian ethics we may surely say that, if this inconceivably vast and complicated process has come to consciousness on this tiny planet by a series of infinitely improbable stellar events, then what happens in that consciousness is of vastly greater importance than the movements of any number of billions of galaxies in space. We have, of course, no right to assume that the entire cosmic process had no other purpose than to produce in one little corner for a brief flicker of time the creature called man. Nor can we exclude the possibility — some would say, the probability — that elsewhere in the universe similar, or even more astonishingly complex and self-conscious beings have appeared, or will appear. The faith on which our Christian ethics rests demands no dogmatic assertions about what may, or may not, be in the infinite mysteries of Space-time. It simply finds in the revelations of modern science more, and not less, reason to consider the significance of man, and the consequent all-importance of his decisions, his actions, and his goals. These are now assuming even greater significance as man extends his range of action beyond the boundaries of this planet, and surely no one is prepared to say that the Christian categories of justice, goodness and love lose their significance for the inhabitants of space-platforms or for the first colonizers of the moon. What ethical problems would be created by an encounter still farther off with intelligent, self-conscious beings, like and unlike ourselves, cannot possibly be anticipated.

It is part of Christian ethics in this age of space also to reject the fears of man's new journey into the unknown, the defeatism that abandons all hope of achieving a healthier society of order and tranquillity, and the surrender to the so-called anonymous powers of automation and robotry.

The Judaeo-Christian tradition contains the doctrine of man's dominion that finds expression in the Genesis story—"And God blessed them, and God said unto them, Be fruitful and multiply, and replenish the earth, and subdue it: and have dominion . . ." (Gen. 1. 28). "The heaven," said the psalmist, "even the heavens are the Lord's: but the earth hath he given to the children of men" (Ps. 115. 16)—and we should have no exegetical qualms in extending "the earth" to such immediate environment of our stellar system as may come within reach. (We might note, incidentally, that although we are promised that "the sun shall not smite thee by day, nor the moon by night" (Ps. 121. 6) there is no prohibition against our smiting the moon!) Christian history is full of examples of a timidity that bears the name of reverence. Objections have been raised on religious grounds to nearly every advance of mankind into new territory, whether through exploration of distant lands, or human ancestry, or the human body, or the recesses of the mind and soul. At this point of rapid and bewildering advance, Christian ethics needs more than ever to assert the biblical truth of man's dominion, based on his unique significance as a creature made in the image of God.

We have then to interpret the whole contemporary movement of mankind with its convergence of nations and multiplication of population, its spectacular dangers and hopes, its concentration of power, its growing planetary self-consciousness, in terms of the responsibility and freedom implied in the Christian ethic. There is no impersonal power that spells out the doom of the human race. It is man who chooses how to use the nuclear power he has unleashed. It is man who decides whether his increasing collectivization shall mean an enlargement or a shrinking of human freedom. It is, and always will be, man who invents and uses the machine — and not vice versa. It is the human mind which decides how to programme the computer. Whether or not Teilhard de Chardin was right in his optimistic estimate of the future course of events — that the next stage of evolution would be the enlarged awareness of mankind, a greater freedom in a greater interpenetration of mind and spirit, and that the struggles and agonies of this generation are the birth-pangs of a happier and warless world — there is no question that Christian ethics demands a restatement of man's responsibility and moral capability at this hour.

So far we have been thinking chiefly of the assertions of our ethical tradition over against the current sense of *insignificance*. But we have also to reckon with the complementary and paradoxical sense of what might be called *omnipotence*. For just as there is a widespread feeling that the ordinary man or woman is of absolutely no account in this immense universe, and that their lives have little meaning or value in a mechanized world, so there is a parallel sensation in other minds of almost unlimited power and control. This is not confined to the breasts of the wielders of power in the presidencies and pentagons of the world, but finds expression in common thought and conversation. A New York taxi-driver remarked to me after one of the first successful orbits of the earth: "Nature's just a little fella after all. We've got it licked." There is no question that the sense of powerlessness and awe that possessed our ancestors before the phenomena of nature has been heavily diluted by the triumphs of applied science. Man seems well on his way to the mastery of secrets that used to be considered sacrosanct. The intoxication of such power can be widespread in days of mass-communication. The sense of omnipotence may indeed be much stronger in those who partake of the triumphs of modern science at second-hand; for the great scientists themselves are humbly aware of the very short journey they have made into the mysteries of creation.

If we take the Genesis symbol of the Tower of Babel as signifying man's assertion of omnipotence, where do we find our Babels in modern society? We have to look in more than one direction. There is the political Babel represented by ideologies that claim to possess the system that will solve man's problems on earth, and out into space. There are the philosophical Babels that erect structures of thought in which no moral restraints are accepted for mankind. There are the psychological Babels that profess to know a norm for human life, based not on ethics but statistics, towards which mankind can be steered. These Babels are reared on the proposition that man has now become totally independent, without need of tutelage or restraint from any supernatural source. And, strangely enough, it seems at the moment as though such Babels were being given a qualified blessing by some voices of modern theology.

It is one thing to face frankly the deliverance of mankind from the chains of superstition and the tendency to call upon God to supply the gaps in our understanding, or the needs of our extremities. It is quite another to state, without qualification, that we must now learn to live "as though there were no God". Such an expression from the pen of a Bonhoeffer, tragically cut short in the midst of his most creative reflexion on Christian ethics and belief, is very different from its repetition in another context and without his profundity and complexity of thought. That other current phrase "religionless Christianity", which is readily understandable by those familiar with the thinking of Karl Barth and other Christ-centred theologians and which has served as a kind of warning-signal against all attempts to turn Christianity into a system of rites and creeds whereby man reaches God, is now being interpreted to mean a Christian way of life that requires no active belief in a personal God. Such a conception is not only a departure from the traditional ethic of the Church; it is impossible to square with the plain teaching of the New Testament.

If the tragic sense of insignificance that has been forced on many minds by the discoveries and applications of modern science can only be countered by a reaffirmation of the true Christian doctrine of man — made in the image of God with creative powers and capacity for true decision — then the sense of omnipotence must be met by a resolute affirmation of the true Christian doctrine of God, the ultimate source of all our ethics. At this point we are told that the Church's traditional teaching about God has become irrelevant and meaningless in this age of scientific understanding and cosmic exploration.

It must be freely granted that no way of thinking or talking about God can ever be either adequate or accurate. This is no new theological discovery. "My thoughts are not your thoughts, neither are your ways my ways, saith the Lord" (Isa. 55. 8). What the author of Second Isaiah expressed was clearly also the attitude of St. Paul, for after his valiant attempt to wrestle through the problem of God's dealing with Israel in the light of the Christian Gospel, he ended with the confession: "O the depth of the riches both of the wisdom and knowledge of God! how unsearchable are his judgments, and his ways past finding out! For who hath known the mind of the Lord? or who hath been his counsellor?" (Rom. 11. 33, 34). While we have to admit that from time to time Christian theologians have appeared who seemed entirely acquainted with the mind of the Lord, and Christian preachers who might almost have served as his counsellors, the plain record of traditional theology from Scriptural days to the present shows that God has never been held to be a kind of Superman, easily understood and fitted into a primitive picture of the universe. There must always be an element of mystery in our apprehension of the God who speaks through the Bible, and a use of imagery and myth in our attempts to declare him.

There is thus no such entirely new problem confronting the believer today as he contemplates his God in this age of space, and there is no greater difficulty in deriving our ethical guidance from the divine than there was for any previous generation. If we are told often enough that in the old superstitious days God was conceived to be a Father-figure literally inhabiting a fixed point in the blue heavens above us, and that in more recent semi-superstitious days he was believed to dwell in a vaguer way somewhere beyond the limits of the visible world, we shall probably come to believe it. If we are prepared to believe that while we may use figurative speech without fear of being taken literally, biblical and classical Christian writers invariably expected to be understood in the crassest literalism, then we shall accept the need for a total rejection of their ways of thought and expression. But if we actually listen, with at least a little sympathetic imagination, to what the scriptural writers are really saying, in the totality of the biblical revelation we shall find that the God of whom they speak is as conceivable in the framework of our world-picture as of any other in the past.

There are innumerable passages in the Bible where the omnipresence of God is indicated in imagery that does not date. "Thus saith the high and lofty One that inhabiteth eternity, whose name is Holy; I dwell in the high and holy place, with him also that is of a contrite and humble spirit . . ." (Isa. 57. 15). "Whither shall I go from thy spirit? or whither shall I flee from thy presence?" (Ps. 139. 7). Or the words of Solomon at the dedication of his Temple: "Behold, the heaven and heaven of heavens cannot contain thee; how much less this house that I have builded?" (1 Kings 8. 27). It is extraordinary in view of the insistence of both Old and New Testaments on the unlimited and unlocated presence of God, and of his responsibility, not just for this or that strange occurrence but for the sum total of things, that contemporary man should be told that he has outgrown Bible ideas about an Old Man in the sky, who occasionally makes his presence felt. The God of whom the Bible speaks, the God of the classical creeds and confessions, the God of our fathers, is still everywhere or nowhere, is still the ultimate meaning of all existence or quite imaginary, is still the final goal of mankind or sheer myth. And so the ethics of outer space either depend on him or they do not exist at all.

The choice before mankind is exactly the same in the nuclear age as it was in the stone age. Either our course of action is bounded by a response to the revelation of God or it is entirely unrestricted. Either we are responsible for our behaviour to a supreme authority or we are not. The biblical answer to man's sense of omnipotence remains in full force: "The fool hath said in his heart, There is no God" (Ps. 14. 1). That answer has clear references not to some theoretical argument about the existence of God, but to the conduct of life. Whether we are dealing with tribes in the desert or modern megalopolis, with spears and javelins or thermo-nuclear weapons,with the crossing of Jordan or flights to the moon, the only final answer to the tragic delusions of omnipotence is the humble acknowledgment of God. Without it, in Bible days and in ours, the vacuum in the human soul will be filled with the idols of man's devising.

There is perhaps more difficulty for modern man in conceiving of the place and authority of Jesus Christ in this revolutionary age.

If our ethics derive from him, it is asked, how can they possibly be adequate for an environment containing so many elements of which the first century was totally unaware? And what, it may further be reasonably asked, is the significance for those worlds unknown where life like ours may conceivably exist, of a figure from a specific era on this tiny planet?

To these questions no one will have complete and satisfying answers, but there are three comments that ought to be made.

(1) The ethics of Jesus Christ, as we have seen, did not consist in the elaboration of a set of rules to cover all the circumstances of human life in his day. They consisted in the response we are asked to make to the love of God as revealed and declared in him. Therefore each age, including ours, has to discover the content of the *Agape* in our own situation. Moral values are not, in their essence, subject to change and decay like suits of clothes, or scientific manuals. We cannot imagine that an astronaut who finds that the law of gravity has been suspended in his capsule would expect to discover that the law of love had also ceased to apply.

(2) When we come to consider what the validity might be of the way of Christ on some planet in another galaxy where conscious beings resided in communities with some resemblance to ours, the only honest answer is that we do not know. How could we possibly know what plans the Almighty has for all the infinite reaches of his creation? The Christian affirms that for this human race the Word of God is Jesus Christ as the Way, the Truth, and the Life. That is all he needs to know.

(3) It must finally, however, be noted that the New Testament contains some striking passages about the cosmic significance of Christ. Since Christian ethics is not simply a matter of discovering what Jesus taught and trying to follow in his steps, but an identification with a Lord and Saviour in whom we find forgiveness and new being, we cannot close this reflection on our age of space without some effort to understand what is meant by "the measure of the stature of the fulness of Christ" (Eph. 4. 13). "He is the image of the invisible God," said St. Paul, "his is the primacy over all created things. In him everything in heaven and on earth was created, not only things visible but also the invisible orders of thrones, sovereignties, authorities, and powers: the whole universe has been created through him and for him. And he exists before everything, and all things are held together in him"

(Col. I. 15–17, *N.E.B.*). Emil Brunner, with the thought of Christ's cosmic significance as the God-man in mind, writes in his *Christianity and Civilization*: "Nothing that astro-physical science has brought or will bring to light about the structure of this Universe, and nothing that biological science has discovered or will discover about the connection between sub-human and human organisms, can shake or even touch this truly Christian theanthropocentrism. If it is true that God created man in his image, and that this image is realized in Christ's God-manhood – and faith knows this to be true – then nothing, either in the sphere of nature or in that of history, can uproot this humanism, unless it be the loss of this faith."

Chapter Eight

THE CHALLENGE OF CHANGE

IT is typical of our age that anyone writing a book on Christian Ethics is sure to find that when he comes to write the last chapter his thoughts on the subject have undergone some changes since he first set pen to paper. No sensitive Christian writer or preacher today can be content to reproduce, month after month, the thoughts he has assembled at some formative period in the past, as if all he had to do was to find contemporary language and illustration for convictions that were settled long ago. He may feel that basically his attitude to God and his fellow men is unchanged. The obligation of love is not subject to question by the whims of time. But new problems are raised and new possibilities open up as the world spins into the future with the fantastic acceleration of recent days. Love must find new interpretation and expression.

It is the speed of change in our generation that has provoked the storm of controversy about the traditional teaching of the Church. Everything is moving so fast — scientific discovery and its practical application, events and their impact through almost instantaneous communication, ideas and their rigid dissemination — that any institution with its roots in the past, like the Church, is bound to be under strain. As the guardian of certain traditional values, and the exponent of a way of life expressed in documents two thousand years old, she is confronted with two simultaneous dangers: of withdrawing into a fortress of established conviction and thus being by-passed by the modern world, and of merging with the stream in a desperate effort to be "relevant" and thus losing her identity. So we find two extreme notes being sounded in the current controversy about Christian ethics.

On the one side there are shrill sounds of alarm from those who believe that the pace of events is dragging society from its moorings. They feel that the very fact of almost universal change makes it all the more necessary to assert that there is one area — of moral and spiritual values — where nothing has changed. They want the

Churches to stand firm as the bastions of traditional morality, and are shocked by deviation from the accepted code or by any suggestion that the inherited system of values is open to question. It is normally the older generation who express such fear of change, and draw doleful comparisons with the "good old days". Yet in times of confusion like these even the young are susceptible to this panic and a minority are always attracted to religious or political movements that offer the kind of certainties they crave. Sheer weariness with the restless debate and absence of strong guide-posts is driving some towards any group that claims to know without ambiguity what is right and what is wrong. So we have the paradox that a period of sweeping change breeds a moral rigidity and an intense conservatism in thought and action.

On the other side, however, we are hearing radical voices of dissent and disturbance. A growing number of churchmen are proposing such a total reshaping of traditional Christian morality that little seems to be left of the codes that were honoured in the past. Books are written, or reports issued, that startle the general public by their repudiation of hitherto accepted Christian standards of conduct, especially in the area of sex. Clergymen make headlines by denouncing the Ten Commandments as a rule of life, or by declaring that the changing times demand a revision of moral values. The assumption is made that, since everything else is in the melting-pot, ethics must share the same fate. The Augustinian aphorism — "Love God and do what you will" — is made the key to all ethical decision, and this at a time when radical theologians of the same school are rapidly evacuating the words "Love of God" of any real meaning. The tempo of modern life dictates the answers that Christians are thus supposed to give to the dilemmas of personal and social conduct. From this view there are no absolute standards whatever. The "situation" governs everything, and the answers that are given, though based on what is called "love", begin to sound more like a majority vote. In other words, while the traditionalist seems to be saying, "What they are all doing is almost certainly wrong", the radical seems to assume "What they are all doing is probably right."

Between these two extremes lies the majority of puzzled people in this swirling world. And since the extremes have the headlines, their confusion deepens. Is the choice really between digging into the prepared positions of conventional morality, and abandoning all standards whatever? It might be helpful for the layman to be reminded that the majority of Christian thinkers today are neither hopeless obscurantists nor wild revolutionaries in the ethical debate. And it is part of the purpose of this book to suggest a point of view that can be both nearer to the New Testament and more immediately helpful than either of the two extremes. Both in ethics and in theology the danger of the central position is that it breeds a certain complacency and inertia. What is needed in this period of rapid change is surely a "dynamic middle" – an ethical and theological conviction that expresses both a loyalty to the Christian Gospel and a sensitivity to the unique needs of our age. There are few of the clergy in Europe and America today who would want to respond to the changing world with a mere reiteration of the moral slogans of past generations; there are still fewer who would sling them all on the rubbish-heap. Our task, then, is to understand and evaluate our moral inheritance, and to translate it into dynamic action in our revolutionary age.

In the words of St. Paul we are called to "prove all things; hold fast that which is good" (1 Thess. 5. 21). Proving – in the sense of testing – all things no doubt referred in its original context to the scrutiny of contemporary outpourings in the early Church. There was considerable diversity then too in the understanding of the Gospel and the practice of Christian ethics, and the apostle was warning against a too-facile acceptance of seductive teachings. But the emphasis is also on the open mind that is ready to listen and to evaluate, and we may legitimately extend the meaning of the words to cover the notion of Christian tolerance and receptivity to new ideas. It was the same apostle who wrote, "All (things) are yours; and ye are Christ's; and Christ is God's" (1 Cor. 3. 22, 23). This note of freedom and enlargement is in marked contrast with the thinking of those whose response to an era of revolutionary change is entirely negative, and who are inclined to reject rather than to "test all things". The unfortunate impression has often been given that Christian ethics consists of a closed body of moral maxims, the acceptance of which spares us from thinking about any new factors that may emerge. The Churches thus appear to many as mere bulwarks of the *status quo,* not really testing the new ideas that are in the modern air, but rejecting them out of hand.

If the words "I am come that they might have life, and that they might have it more abundantly" (John 10. 10) describe the true impact of Christ on the human spirit, then clearly this rejection of new thought and experience is a distortion of the Gospel. "All things" are the heritage of the Christian, in the sense that he is summoned to open his mind to all new truth from whatever direction it comes, and his soul to the treasures of an expanding universe. A church that is alive to the Spirit is not afraid of revolutionary ideas for, by his Spirit, God is the Lord of the future and the Source of the new. The failure of the conventional guardians of Christian morals to present the religion that inspires them as an enlargement rather than a restriction accounts for the suspicion with which the younger generation regards the pronouncements of both parents and Church. The so-called "youth revolt", with its slogan "Never trust anyone over thirty", implies a rejection of what seems a hypocritical honouring of moral standards that are not, in fact, observed. The older generation, inside and outside the Church, is seen as clinging to a restrictive morality based on the demands of an ancient God in whom they do not really believe. If we could recapture the biblical image of God as the living, creative Power — the God who, because he is ageless, is infinitely young as well as infinitely old; if we could present Christ as the enlarger of our experience and the transformer of our values; if we realized in action the Holy Spirit as the dynamic of true change: then Christian ethics might have a different sound and flavour for the rising generation.

Those who are saying that the conventional ethics of the Judaeo-Christian tradition are rapidly becoming irrelevant in the modern world usually have in mind some rather parochial version of "moral behaviour". There *is* a morality that is primarily restrictive and backward-looking. There *is* a mentality that is scared by the challenges of a changing world. But the ethical tradition of western civilization cannot be equated with any local and temporary pattern of morality; nor can it be said that Christian ethics has always been a matter of being recalled to "the good old days". A glance at Christian history in perspective will soon show that biblical religion has given rise to a very wide variety of cultures in which no standardized system of morality can be distinguished. The ethical norms of an eighteenth-century Scottish village were not those of fifteenth-century Florence, or twentieth-century Chicago, or the first-century Church at Corinth. Yet each of these societies has been shaped by the Christian ethic.

It must also be confessed without camouflage that the Churches have more than once shifted their stance on questions of right and wrong. What was said about such matters as usury, or birth control in one generation has been contradicted in the next. And it is notorious that it took about eighteen hundred years for slavery to be generally recognized as unconditionally wrong. What this indicates is not that Christian ethics is so flexible as to be virtually meaningless, but that it contains a dynamic element that responds to new situations, and never imposes a uniformity of behaviour at times and places. The morality of the Spirit is capable of great variety of expression, and of expanding to meet "all things" as the changing world brings them to view. The theology of the Spirit implies a built-in critique of every accepted code of behaviour in any age or place.

To recognize this dynamism in Christian ethics is, however, very far from the assertion that all standards and norms can be scrapped while we await the guidance of the Spirit for each particular situation as it arises. The advocates of so-called "situational ethics" are apt to speak as if this generation of churchmen had made the astonishing discovery that living by Love is more Christian than living by Law. It is, of course, the central message of the New Testament — incarnated in Christ and expounded by St. Paul — but in both Gospels and Epistles the way of Love is not presented as a totally "new" morality. Love is seen as the fulfilment of the Law and not its negation. Hence the first Christians, while testing all things, held fast to that which was good. Jesus never spoke as though the Ten Commandments had no validity for those who accepted his Way. His freedom from legalism, his assertion of the primacy of compassion, his rejection of a merely external moralism, cannot be interpreted to mean that he was totally abrogating the ethical tradition of Judaism. On the contrary he repeatedly reaffirmed it, raising the demands for honesty, purity, integrity, respect for the neighbour, filial piety, to an infinite degree. According to St. Matthew he said: "Whosoever therefore shall break one of these least commandments, and shall teach men so, he shall be called the least in the kingdom of heaven" (Matt. 5. 19). Reference is often made to his compassionate treatment of the woman taken in adultery, and there are few more moving stories of his devastating rebuke to the hardhearted and the hypocritical. But it is not so often noted that the story ends with the words: "Go, and sin no more" (John 8. 11). For him, if not for modern moralists, it was possible to act in sovereign love while holding fast the principle that adultery is sin.

In the same way we find St. Paul, while struggling to express the new liberty he had found in Christ, holding fast to the ethical absolutes of right and wrong. He has so many different things to say about the Law, ranging from apparent rejection ("ye are not under the law, but under grace" [Rom. 6. 14]) to emphatic acceptance ("Wherefore the law is holy, and the commandment holy, and just, and good" [Rom. 7. 12]) that it has sometimes been supposed that his conversion was incomplete, that he was a Christian still wrestling with his Pharisaic training. But it is plain that he was following the teaching of his Lord as he expressed the relationship of Law and Love. "For this, Thou shalt not commit adultery, Thou shalt not kill, Thou shalt not steal, Thou shalt not bear false witness, Thou shalt not covet; and if there be any other commandment, it is briefly comprehended in this saying, namely, Thou shalt love thy neighbour as thyself. Love worketh no ill to his neighbour: therefore love is the fulfilling of the law" (Rom. 13. 9, 10). To hold that St. Paul stopped half-way in his moral revolution, that he should have boldly announced that there is no moral law but only the obligation to love, is hardly an advance in ethical insight. For this was precisely the attitude of the "antinomians" in his own day who, on the strength of his doctrine of grace, permitted themselves all kinds of licence and excess. The Church has already had experience of what can happen if moral standards are scorned in the name of an all-permissive "love".

The average Christian may be excused for feeling that this is entirely the wrong time for the Church to appear to be hesitant about asserting ethical norms, and occasionally blatant in defence of sub-normal behaviour. Granted that Christian ethics are not to be identified with what used to be conventional Anglo-Saxon middle-class morality, and granted that we have often given a warped impression of the scope and emphases of the real New Testament standards, surely the trend of the times calls for resistance to current amorality rather than an echo. In the desperate search for "relevance" today's clergy often seem to be straining to prove that they can more than keep up with the secular world in theological scepticism and moral relativism. Hence the aversion from what is called "God-talk" is paralleled by a muting of "ought-talk". All that we are supposed to say about God is that he is not the Person whom our fathers trusted, and the only moral imperative is that to acknowledge moral absolutes is wrong. There is no living God, and we ought not to believe in any "oughts".

This line of thought, which is more than confusing to the average layman, should not be accepted as the "wave of the future". While it is true that a merely conventional Christian ethic, based on the values of the Victorian era, is inadequate for the age through which we are speeding, it should not be assumed that Christianity will only survive by rapid adjustment to the current climate of secular opinion. Nor is its strength to be measured by its skill in adapting to the popular demand for more and more permissive codes of behaviour. On the contrary, history has shown that once an institution loses its distinctive *raison d'être* it is doomed to merge without trace into the surrounding culture. If the Church in any part of the world ceases to stand for any particular belief about God or any consequent sense of moral obligation, or way of living, it will soon belong not to the future but to the past. It is simply not true that Christianity has progressed by a continual slackening of its theology and loosening of its moral demands. Just as moral and theological renewal happened in Old Testament times through the appearance of prophets who were consistently in strong opposition to the trend of their times, so the Church has advanced whenever genuine belief has been renewed and new moral insights asserted, whether they have been in tune with the times or not. It is never a question of simply returning to the convictions of a previous age, and it is also never a question of merely adjusting to the current secular mood. So neither "reactionaries", who strive to reverse the clock, nor "progressives", who echo the prevailing opinion, are going to set the pace for the Church of the future.

The reality of the Holy Spirit as the divine Contemporary remains the key to Christian ethics in this, as in any other generation. "As many as are led by the Spirit of God," says St. Paul, "they are the sons of God" (Rom. 8. 14). The idea of being led implies the conviction, often forgotten, that our God is ahead of us. Somehow the notion is rooted in men's minds that to look for divine guidance means always looking to the past. But Christian ethics has an eschatological thrust. To quote another apostle:

"Now are we the sons of God, and it doth not yet appear what we shall be: but we know that, when he shall appear, we shall be like him; for we shall see him as he is" (1 John 3. 2). The ethical ideal in the New Testament is set before us, not just as an unknown to be achieved in an eternal dimension beyond the bounds of this life, but as a goal to which we can be moving now. The ministry of the Church is given "till we all come in the unity of the faith, and of the knowledge of the Son of God, unto a perfect man, unto the measure of the stature of the fulness of Christ" (Eph. 4. 13). The Christian therefore lives not only by the light of the Incarnation thrown, as it were, from behind, but by the light of the *Parousia* that shines from the ultimate fulfilment of all history in Christ. It is the Spirit who beckons us towards this future, and who opens up the new insights that are needed for each generation, and for each stage in our personal life as Christians. It is as true for ethics as it is for theology that "when he, the Spirit of truth, is come, he will guide you into all truth" (John 16. 13). It is in response to the Holy Spirit, and not to the spirit of the times, that the Church and the individual Christian rides the "wave of the future".

What is needed in a time of bewildering change and disintegration of traditional moralities is both a sensitivity to the beckoning of the Spirit *and* a reaffirmation of the validity of the divine law. It may be that "law" is in some ways a misleading metaphor; it suggests to many the notion of a celestial book of rules covering all possible contingencies, complete with appropriate rewards and penalties. In the Bible the word is used in no such cold and impersonal context. It is the living will of God, spelled out in terms of human conduct. It evokes not only respect, but devotion and enthusiasm. "O how love I thy law!" cries the psalmist, "it is my meditation all the day" (Ps. 119. 97). Again, "The statutes of the Lord are right, rejoicing the heart: the commandment of the Lord is pure, enlightening the eyes" (Ps. 19. 8). Perhaps God's Way, rather than Law, would convey the biblical thought, which is very far from a prosaic legalism. But the important point is that there *is* such a way, that there *is* such a will of God that has been revealed for all mankind. St. Paul, believing firmly in the unique revelation of God's law to the Jewish people, also teaches that "When Gentiles who do not possess the law carry out its precepts by the light of nature, then, although they have no law, they are their own law, for they display the effect of the law inscribed on their hearts" (Rom. 2. 14, 15, *N.E.B.*). The precise content of this law, or will of God for men, is not conveyed in a series of rules, covering all areas of human behaviour: that would rob our life of all spontaneity and entirely destroy the personal communion with God that is the heart of the Christian life. But this is far from saying that there is no concrete Law to be observed, no clear statement to be made about God's will. The question: "What doth the Lord require of thee?" was not left unanswered. "He hath shewed thee, O man, what is good ... to do justly, and to love mercy, and to walk humbly with thy God" (Mic. 6. 8). It is this will of God for us, this way of life, that is reflected in such plain precepts as those we know as the Ten Commandments.

These Commandments are, of course, to be read in their historical context, and understood in the light of Christ. (It is not very helpful to have their promulgation depicted by Hollywood in the shape of a magical electrode sizzling out of the storm on to the rock of Mount Sinai.) But the content surely remains unmistakable — unswerving loyalty to God, and worship of him alone, filial respect, prohibition of murder, adultery, theft, lying, and covetousness. To affirm the Law is to uphold the validity of such standards for all men and for all times. They are the frame of reference in which ethical decisions are made within the Judaeo–Christian tradition. It is absurd to suppose that the guidance of the Law, in this sense, can be thrown aside and every decision made in spontaneous response to the Spirit of God. Those who claim that the Christian can view with equanimity the collapse of such standards, since our only final obligation is to act in love, ignore the immense part played by the concept of moral law both in determining the tone of the society in which we live and in the practical decision of every day. Life is not, after all, made up of a series of great choices in which we deliberately choose to act in response to the prompting of the Spirit in the context of loving concern. Such moments are comparatively rare; our character is formed in a multitude of almost instinctive decisions and these are determined by the moral code in which we have been trained, modified perhaps by our own experience and reflection. The place of the Law as the basic moral structure of society and as the normal source of guidance and inspiration for the individual is seriously underestimated in the current schools of "contextual ethics" —

when by "context" is meant simply the unique situation in which a decision is made. The New Testament knows of these unique situations too, but never suggests that the whole of morality consists in the spontaneous response at the moment of challenge. The parable of the Good Samaritan tells of such a response—a demonstration of *Agape* in action; but you will notice that it comes as an illustration of the Law. "What is written in the law?" "Thou shalt love the Lord thy God with all thy heart, and with all thy soul, and with all thy strength, and with all thy mind; and thy neighbour as thyself." "Thou hast answered right: this do, and thou shalt live." (Luke 10. 26–8). We should not surely be wrong in supposing that the instinctive response of the Samaritan in the context of his neighbour's need rose out of his knowledge of, and respect for, the Law of God. It is worth remarking that the first Christians, with all their pristine enthusiasm for the freedom of the Gospel, and their sensitivity to the immediate guidance of the Spirit, found it necessary to instruct converts in the Law of God and to make it an integral part of their worship.

Those who are summoning us to reject all absolute standards except the law of love are fond of citing examples of moral dilemmas in which the truly "Christian" solution seems to be the breaking of one of the Ten Commandments. We are told that the pace of human progress has rendered obsolete any fixed principles, and that the Church is now being challenged to declare openly that so-called moral standards were simply the reflexion of the prejudices of a particular stage in human development and have no objective validity. This thesis is usually illustrated by case histories in which the apparently right thing to do in a particular context was to steal, to lie, to commit adultery, or to kill. Since the essence of the "new morality" seems to be the insistence that these cases prove that there is no absolute moral law beyond that of love, it is worth examining what is really implied by these dilemmas. Three observations can be made:

(1) There is nothing whatever radically new, or even startling, in the discovery that life occasionally faces the Christian with situations when it seems impossible—or even wrong—to comply with the normal requirements of traditional morality. We are not the first generation to face the dilemma of the "white lie", or "legitimate killing", or "emergency stealing". The writer once

heard a discussion on the subject "Is it ever right to tell a lie?" by some German theological students in 1946. They were unanimous in answering in the negative. Then an old lady who was present spoke up. "Last year", she said, "my home in the east was invaded by the Russian army. My granddaughter, aged seventeen, was hiding in the attic. Some drunken soldiers broke in and asked me: 'Are there any girls in here?' I said: 'No.' Was I wrong?" Silence fell, and the discussion was over. Every moral theologian from the first century has been aware of this kind of dilemma, and many kinds of answers have been devised. Even more profuse has been the debate about the legitimacy of killing, especially in war, and again the answers have taken different forms. We may accept one or the other of the solutions to these dilemmas that have been offered by conscientious Christian thinkers, but what we cannot do is to pretend that these dilemmas are forced upon us by the revolutionary age in which we live and must now be answered by a categoric repudiation of the concept of a moral law. There has been no fundamental change in the situation of the Christian who is confronted with these agonizing questions. The only change seems to be in the conclusions which some now appear willing to draw from them.

(2) A protest ought surely now to be made that a concentration on these extreme instances of moral ambiguity throws our consideration of Christian ethics out of perspective. Just how often in the course of one man's life is he faced with the apparent need to break one of the Commandments? (We are talking about *need* — in Christian conscience — not just of inclination.) Morality is concerned with the whole range of human life, seeking to offer guidance to society and the individual, and one might easily reach the end of one's days without even being caught in one of these exceptional dilemmas. At a time when the entire basis of public and private morality is threatened with erosion and collapse it is extraordinary to find such emphasis being placed on the extreme cases that have been known to the Church from the beginning, and from which no devastating conclusions can be drawn. A theologian, or preacher, may find it fascinating to discuss some hypothetical case in which the dictates of *Agape* seem to suggest the contravention of a "moral law", and he may be aware of all the theological debate that has surrounded such dilemmas throughout the history of the Church. But he should not

be surprised to find himself featured next day in the press under such headlines as: "Cleric Says Lying is O.K." or "Church Leader Condones Adultery." The business of Christian ethics is primarily with the practical questions of everyday life, the shaping of character, and the provision of some ethical norms of behaviour, and not with theoretical discussion of isolated cases of extreme ambiguity. Such cases do, of course, require an answer, but in an age of extreme confusion and rapidly changing mores the Christian Church should be chiefly concerned with the affirmation of the way of life that is based on the recognition of moral standards that have their sanction and their roots in God.

(3) We must, however, face the fact that there are some areas of modern life where we seem to be constantly confronted with the impossibility of a literal obedience to the law of God in the traditional sense of the Ten Commandments, expanded and illuminated by the teachings of Christ. These have chiefly to do with questions of sex and war. The dilemma does *not* arise from the normal human resistance to the Commandments that enjoin marital faithfulness or the loving of one's enemies. In spite of our temptations there is nothing to prevent such faithfulness even in a time of sexual permissiveness, or such an attitude to one's enemies even in time of war, It is, in fact, such obedience in spite of the prevailing moral climate, that distinguishes the Christian way of life. The problem arises when we face such questions as the re-marriage of divorced persons in the light of Christ's declaration (Mark 10. 11), or participation in war in the light of the Commandment "Thou shalt not kill". It is, of course, theoretically possible to take an absolutist position and attempt to refuse recognition of either divorce or war. But the demands of justice in both cases have constantly led to a modification of the strict rule in practice, and it is clear that in modern conditions it is entirely impossible to "have nothing to do" with either divorce or war — short of living in some distant Shangri-La. Attempts to maintain a rigorist position break down in face of the realities. In the question of divorce an effort may be made to prove that the original marriage lacked some element to give it ecclesiastical validity, and therefore was not a marriage at all. The pacifist has to find some stance where he can "conscientiously object" to war, but where is that to be — at the point of combatant service, non-combatant service, involvement in industry geared to war, or payment of taxes?

The theological discipline of casuistry was developed in order to maintain the integrity of the moral law while taking account of the occasions when we seem forced to break it. Thus, the re-marriage of a divorced person could be held to be consonant with the rule of one wife "till death do us part" provided it could be demonstrated that the original marriage was ecclesiastically invalid. Similarly a doctrine of the "Just War" was formulated to prove that in certain circumstances participation in war is no violation of the Commandment against taking human life. (It was in any case obvious that in Old Testament times the Commandment referred to murder and not to either warfare or capital punishment.) Casuistry — in spite of the semantic disrepute into which it has fallen — is at its best a noble effort to satisfy the Christian conscience and offer guidance in those choices where there seems to be no black or white, but only shades of grey. It deals normally, not with these questions of divorce and war about which the Roman Catholic Church, for example, has an explicit body of teaching, but with personal decisions in conditions of extreme moral ambiguity. A concrete example is a question that was raised with the writer in a P.O.W. camp during World War II: "Is it wrong for us to tell a lie to a German guard?" One answer that had been given was: "No; because as your enemy he has no right to the truth." A preferable answer is surely: "Lying is wrong: therefore never lie unless you have to." The "unless you have to" may sound cynical, but is in fact the recognition that circumstances might arise when a lie was the only way to shield a life or prevent a tragedy.

These reflections point to a conclusion that is of cardinal importance for Christian ethics. It is expressed in the familiar phrase about "choosing the lesser of two evils". Experience teaches us that we are not, in every situation, faced with a choice between right and wrong. There are times when the only options are between different degrees of wrong. A clear case for most Christians would be such a situation as the outbreak of World War II. On the one hand a sensitive conscience knows that war is evil, that it cannot be waged without injustice and hideous suffering, that it breeds hatreds, lies, enduring bitterness, and appalling cruelties. On the other hand the same conscience at that time had to reckon with the consequences for all mankind of the extension of Nazi tyranny and demonic ideology. The majority of Christians, whether with grim deliberation or almost instinctively, decided that the latter was the worse of two evils. The cynic may say that when any war comes along the Churches of any nation have been quick to decide that the national cause takes precedence over any moral hesitations about warfare, and it has to be admitted that the Christian record over the centuries gives us no cause for pride. Yet it is entirely unfair to suggest that the Church, even at the time of World War II, welcomed war as intrinsically good and right. It was seen rather as an evil that had to be accepted since the alternative was something worse. The story of the twenties and thirties is a good example of how collective failure of moral nerve in confronting evil and seeking justice led to a situation where the terrible choice was inevitable.

It is clear that there are other situations — divorce, abortion, the concealment of the truth, civil disobedience, the manufacture of nuclear weapons — where the Christian may find himself confronted with a choice, not between black and white, but between two blacks or shades of grey. A decision must be made, but whatever it is some wrong will be done. This is the agony for the sensitive conscience, and this is also an offence to our pride which demands the white robe of innocence. But there is no such white robe for us so long as we live in a sinful world. The important point here is that this kind of impasse does not invalidate the moral law. Just because, no matter what we do, we are not able perfectly to fulfil it, we have no right to say that it is only a figment of theological imagination. The Commandments stand. The way of life set forth in the Sermon on the Mount remains the eternal will of God for his human family. No wind of change blowing through our world can alter the conviction that God has a constant purpose for all mankind. No theory of progress has ever indicated how we can move beyond its incarnation in Christ to some new morality that transcends his requirement.: "Be ye therefore perfect, even as your Father which is in heaven is perfect" (Matt. 5. 48). There are times when, like our forefathers, we can see no way out of a situation without wrong being done. Therefore, instead of devising some new ethic which makes our action pure, we must rather say with them: "God be merciful to me a sinner" (Luke 18. 13) as we make our decision in faith and love.

It is this predicament that throws us back on the fundamental, and often misunderstood Christian doctrines of sin and grace. If sin is not just an occasional personal shortcoming or moral error, but, as the Bible teaches, an infection that has corrupted the whole human race, then it is made plain why these fearful dilemmas are sure to arise. It is only a generation that really believes itself to have "come of age", in the sense of moral independence and autonomy, that can be deluded into thinking that there must always be a pure, perfect, and right way out of any situation. We can readily admit that the Church has had to adjust to changes in our understanding of man's nature and history, and in our interpretation of the biblical documents. "Original sin" does not mean for most modern theologians a theory of man's depravity based on a single historical act of disobedience in the Garden of Eden. Still less is it held to be linked with the act of procreation. But "original sin" is still used as a term to describe the belief, supported both by the Bible and observable fact, that mankind is radically and pervasively alienated from God. The image of the angel with the flaming sword guarding the way back to the Garden speaks of the impossibility of finding a place of total innocence, a society that is quite uncorrupted and in perfect harmony with the will of God. Such a belief does not involve us in any hopeless pessimism or exaggerated condemnation of the human race. It does not mean that we regard our neighbours as potential criminals or knaves. On the contrary it reminds us that we are *all* — whatever our religion or irreligion — involved in this human predicament, and therefore in need of that reconciling power that the Bible calls "grace".

The *Confession of 1967* of the United Presbyterian Church in the United States of America expresses this understanding of pervasive sin in words which are both scriptural and modern. This is an excellent example of a Church meeting the challenge of change and yet preserving the essential content of a basic doctrine of Faith, entitled "Of the Fall of Man, Sin, and the Punishment thereof".)

"Wise and virtuous men through the ages have sought the highest good in devotion to freedom, justice, peace, truth, and beauty. Yet all human virtue, when seen in the light of God's love in Jesus Christ, is found to be infected by self-interest and hostility. All men, good and bad alike, are in the wrong before God and helpless without his forgiveness. Thus all men fall under God's judgment. No one is more subject to that judgment than the man who assumes he is guiltless before God or morally superior to others." (*The Proposed Book of Confession*, p. 179.)

There is, of course, a danger that this doctrine of sin can be cynically used to excuse both blatant immorality ("I'm just an old sinner, you know," says the tough guy with some residual Calvinism in his bones), and a sceptical indifference to all efforts to remove injustices and promote peace ("You can't change human nature; we'll always have poverty and wars"). Yet nothing, either in the Bible or the history of the Church, can possibly justify drawing this kind of conclusion. This is not a doctrine of pessimism, but of realism; not of resignation, but of resolution. For it is when we realize how serious is this alienation that infects us all that we are driven to seek the solution in God's grace. And it is that grace which, today as in the past, is the motivating power of Christian ethics, the source of hope, and the stimulus to personal and social reform.

The present situation, in fact, would seem to call for a fresh discovery of what is meant by grace even more urgently than it demands a reiteration of the moral law and an understanding of sin. Yet in those ethical and theological "revolutions" that are being proposed to meet the challenge of the modern world the note of grace is strangely absent. What has happened is that, with the disappearance of the transcendental claims of a living God and therefore of any real sense of having "offended against thy holy laws," there is no longer experienced "the promise of redeeming grace, remitting all our sins, and cleansing us from an evil conscience, through the perfect sacrifice of Jesus Christ our Lord". It is this realization of forgiveness and newness of life that has always lain at the heart of Christian ethics, and every renewal and reformation of the Church has been prompted by it. There is no reason to suppose that the renewal will come in this period of change and confusion from any other direction. For grace is precisely the reconciling love of God come alive in the human heart with contemporary power. It is not an old-fashioned doctrine but an up-to-date experience. And it is associated with freedom, with spontaneity, with gratitude, and with joy.

There is enough in current reflections on the world to remind us of sin. A great deal of modern literature and art is devoted, consciously or unconsciously, to a portrayal of the dislocations caused by the mystery of evil in human relations. The artist has taken over from the preacher the task of exposing the dark recesses of the human soul. The psychiatrist has added to our understanding of the convolutions of human behaviour, and has made us more sceptical about our "innocent motives" and purity of heart. The renaissance of cruelty and violence on a vast scale has robbed the average man of his old confidence in the innate decencies of human nature. At such a time the Church is surely challenged, not to add its quota to the diagnoses of evil or to join the chorus of confusion by abandoning the absolutes, but to speak and to act the word of grace. It is the missing word in so much of our current output of literature, theology, philosophy, ethics, and art. Hence the cleverness without conviction, the brilliance without hope, the beauty without joy, the truth without depth. The Church has to find the way of saying in terms of today what the early Church discovered to be the secret of Christian ethics: "Where sin abounded, grace did much more abound" (Rom. 5. 20). This does not mean just finding new words for the pulpit. Grace is spoken where men and women meet in reconciling love, in real encounter, in hopeful enterprise. Grace may come through unexpected channels in the generation pressing behind us – in new freedoms, in new disciplines, in new worship, in new art. Wherever and however it comes it means life and not death, love and not bitterness, hope and not despair, meaning and not absurdity. Grace is not always articulated in conventional words, but wherever it is authentically present it springs from the Gospel of the crucified and risen Christ.

It is difficult to see how there can be any fresh experience of grace in the world that we are rushing into unless there is a real awareness of the living God and his claims upon us. For the reconciling power of the Gospel in personal life and in the great conflicts with which society is torn springs from the fact that "God was in Christ, reconciling the world unto himself" (2 Cor. 5. 19). Throughout the New Testament the love that is the solvent of human ills and stresses is a reflection of the love that God has bestowed upon us. "We love because he loved us first" (1 John 4. 19, *N.E.B.*). This is the keystone of Christian ethics. Our behaviour, our decisions, are not then ultimately based on any code, whether that of the Law, or on the sophisticated versions of law that are being offered in the name of "new morality". The love that determines the Christian style of life is more than humanitarianism, more than dedicated service, more than living for others — though it includes them all. It is the response of one who has received the grace of God, who claims no merit, who refrains from judgment, who seeks to do God's will, and who is joyfully prepared to be led by God's Spirit.

The old analogy holds. Christ calls us to be sons of God. In a good human family a child learns his way by responding to the love that is given him. He knows the rules. Even when of age he does not reject the rules. For the rules are just another expression of parental love. But the heart of the relationship is the personal response of love. So it is with the Christian as he seeks the good life in this confusing age. He responds to the living God as he knows him in Christ, is guided by his law, and inspired by his Spirit. There is an unchanging Centre for the Christian life — "Jesus Christ the same yesterday, and today, and for ever" (Heb. 13. 8). And there is in him, and from him, a Spirit of change to lead us into new truth and action. So in our understanding of Christian ethics in this changing world we would be wise to listen again to the words of the Master: "When, therefore, a teacher of the law has become a learner in the kingdom of Heaven, he is like a householder who can produce from his store both the new and the old." (Matt. 13. 52, *N.E.B.*).

INDEX

BIBLICAL REFERENCES

176 7230